Knowledge and

MW00643701

Jason Stanley presents a startling and provocative claim about knowledge: that whether or not someone knows a proposition at a given time is in part determined by his or her practical interests. Whether a true belief is knowledge is not merely a matter of supporting beliefs or reliability; in the case of knowledge, practical rationality and theoretical rationality are intertwined. Stanley defends this thesis against alternative accounts of the phenomena that motivate it, such as the claim that knowledge attributions are linguistically context-sensitive (contextualism about knowledge attributions), and the claim that the truth of a knowledge claim is somehow relative to the person making the claim (relativism about knowledge).

In the course of his argument Stanley discusses a number of strategies for resolving philosophical paradox, making the book essential not just for specialists in epistemology but for all philosophers interested in philosophical methodology. Since a number of these strategies appeal to linguistic evidence, it will be of great interest to linguists as well.

LINES OF THOUGHT
This series is published in association with the Aristotelian Society.

Jason Stanley is Professor of Philosophy at Rutgers University.

Lines of Thought

Short philosophical books

General editors: Peter Ludlow and Scott Sturgeon
Published in association with the Aristotelian Society

Knowledge and Practical Interests

Jason Stanley

CLARENDON PRESS · OXFORD

OXFORD
UNIVERSITY PRESS

Great Clarendon Street, Oxford OX2 6DP

Oxford University Press is a department of the University of Oxford.
It furthers the University's objective of excellence in research, scholarship,
and education by publishing worldwide in

Oxford New York

Auckland Cape Town Dar es Salaam Hong Kong Karachi
Kuala Lumpur Madrid Melbourne Mexico City Nairobi
New Delhi Shanghai Taipei Toronto

With offices in

Argentina Austria Brazil Chile Czech Republic France Greece
Guatemala Hungary Italy Japan Poland Portugal Singapore
South Korea Switzerland Thailand Turkey Ukraine Vietnam

Oxford is a registered trade mark of Oxford University Press
in the UK and in certain other countries

Published in the United States
by Oxford University Press Inc., New York

British Library Cataloguing in Publication Data

Data available

Library of Congress Cataloging in Publication Data

Data available

Typeset by SPI Publisher Services, Pondicherry, India
Printed in Great Britain
on acid-free paper by
Clays Ltd., St.Ives plc

ISBN 978-0-19-928803-8 (Hbk.)   978-0-19-923043-3 (Pbk.)

1

PREFACE

The thesis of this book is that what makes someone's true belief a case of knowledge is partly determined by facts from the domain of practical rationality. In the senses of 'epistemic' with which most philosophers in the analytic tradition are familiar, the thesis of the book is that the difference between true belief and knowledge is not purely epistemic. I am sympathetic to a similar thesis about our ordinary notions of justification and evidence, though I do not try to establish that further thesis here.

The conclusions I have drawn here are occasionally distressing to me. It has been no comfort at all to realize that friends and family members more at home with non-analytic traditions in philosophy find them unsurprising. My route to these conclusions began with a project on philosophical methodology, of which this book is a part. My philosophical tendency is to preserve as much as possible of common-sense intuition. The goal of this project is to evaluate, in light of this desideratum, appeals to semantic mechanisms (such as context-sensitivity, fictionalism, or truth-relativity) to resolve philosophical problems. In the conclusion of my paper 'Context and Logical Form', I argued that my discussion provided evidence against the thesis that knowledge ascriptions were context-sensitive, a thesis popular among epistemologists. I was also at work on a lengthy paper focusing specifically on evaluating contextualism in epistemology.

Three events led to the broadening of my project. The first was the publication of Delia Graff's paper 'Shifting Sands: An Interest-Relative Theory of Vagueness' in 2000. Graff and I had been discussing context-sensitivity for years, and in her paper she appealed to what she called *interest-relativity* to minimize her appeals to context-sensitivity in presenting her theory of vagueness. I realized she was describing a somewhat general strategy that could allow one to gain some of the benefits of contextualist approaches, but without the semantic costs. But I also realized that the strategy was limited in applicability, and in particular, was quite problematic in her chosen case, that of vagueness. In grappling with her interest-relative theory of vagueness (the result of which appears here in Chapter 9, which contains as a proper part my paper 'Context, Interest-Relativity, and the Sorites' (*Analysis*, 63/4 (2003), 269–80)), I realized that my objections to her interest-relative theory would not apply to an interest-relative theory of knowledge. I then began to think about the prospects for an interest-relative account of knowledge.

The second event was the publication of Timothy Williamson's *Knowledge and its Limits* in 2000. I found the general thrust of Williamson's 'knowledge-first' epistemology extremely persuasive. One unfortunate aspect of traditional epistemology is the tendency to replace natural and intuitive appeals to knowledge by appeals to the 'knowledge-free' notions that were supposed to appear in its analysis. Since I am naturally attracted to preserving common-sense explanations, I was not attracted by much in traditional epistemology. Williamson provided a powerful alternative vision.

One of the most compelling aspects of Williamson's epistemology is that it reminds us how intimately knowledge is bound up with our ordinary practices. An utterly common way to criticize someone's assertion that *p* is to point out that they do not know that *p*, and an utterly common way of criticizing someone's decision to act is to point out that it was based upon a belief that did not amount to knowledge. A natural reaction philosophers have to these points is to attempt to replace ordinary appeals to knowledge by appeals to other notions, such as belief or true belief, and when that fails, to replace such appeals by sophisticated surrogates, such as appropriately confident belief. All such approaches threaten to rob knowledge of the value it obviously seems to have to our common-sense scheme, and thereby to give in to the spirit, if not the letter, of skepticism. At a certain point I realized that the intuitions that led epistemologists to contextualism really should not be explained away by semantic mechanisms. Rather, they were reflections of the connections between knowledge and action, akin to the connections between knowledge and assertion revealed by Moore's Paradox. These intuitions reveal facts about knowledge, and not just facts about 'knowledge'.

The third event was my move to the University of Michigan in the fall of 2000. Once I arrived at Michigan, I immersed myself in a philosophical culture that was rather new to me, one that centered on frameworks for the analysis of practical rationality, as well as the more formal aspects of epistemology. I spent many hours in the offices of my colleagues, particularly Jim Joyce, receiving cost-free tutorials on basic elements of these frameworks. These endless tutorials and seminars (again, particularly by Jim Joyce) gave me the resources to think about an interest-relative theory of knowledge in a considerably more detailed manner. I was not content advocating an interest-relative theory of knowledge unless I could convince myself that the details of such a view would add no more complexity and difficulty than was already present in ordinary analyses of knowledge. So, in Chapter 5 of this book, I present a first-order interest-relative theory of knowledge. Like all analyses of knowledge, the first-order theory of knowledge I provide is incorrect. But the reason it is incorrect has nothing whatever to do with its interest-relative character. Interest-relativity does not add additional unmanageable complexity to epistemology.

The first sketch of what later became this book was a paper I presented in the 2002 University of Massachusetts conference on contextualism in epistemology, organized by Jonathan Schaffer. In that paper I laid out most of the ideas in this book, albeit in embryonic form. Among other things, I laid out some of the criticisms to contextualism that form parts of Chapters 2, 3, and 4, and sketched an interest-relative theory of knowledge. A proper part of this paper was published in the conference proceedings ('On the Linguistic Basis for Contextualism', *Philosophical Studies*, 119: 119–46). After a year or two more of work, I decided that the only way to present the material was in book form. Because of all this, and the additional time it has taken me to convince myself that my views can be worked out satisfactorily, this project has taken me five years to complete, rather than the one year I had planned for it when I started a paper on contextualism in epistemology in the fall of 2000. I apologize to all those who had to listen to numerous different versions of this material. I can only hope that the seemingly endless revision in response to comments has resulted in superior insights.

The interest-relative theory of knowledge must be a natural outgrowth of recent thinking. At the first Kline conference, organized by Jon Kvanvig at the University of Missouri, Columbia, in the fall of 2003, four of the five speakers (me, John Hawthorne, Jeremy Fantl, and Matthew McGrath) were presenting different versions of an interest-relative theory of knowledge. Though I think we all started at the same time, the other defenders of this view have been quicker into print than I have been (Fantl and McGrath 2002; Hawthorne 2004: ch. 4). The end result is that I have benefited from being able to develop the final version of my views with the clarity provided by the efforts of these extremely able philosophers.

I have presented material from this book to numerous audiences, including ones at the University of Massachusetts at Amherst, University of California at Berkeley, University of Southern California, Vassar College, University of Reading,

University of Glasgow, Australian National University, Massachusetts Institute of Technology, Northwestern University, University of Stockholm, Wayne State University, University of Missouri at Columbia, Centro de Filosofia da Universidade de Lisboa, University of Barcelona, University of Oslo, and the Pacific Division of the American Philosophical Association, as well as reading groups and graduate seminars at Oxford University and the University of Michigan. I have learned a great deal from all these encounters.

Individual thanks are due to too many people to list here. Among the more salient are Aaron Bronfman, Herman Cappelen, Jamie Dreier, Allan Gibbard, Thony Gillies, Delia Graff, Richard Heck, Thomas Hofweber, Jon Kvanvig, Ernie Lepore, Peter Ludlow, John MacFarlane, Bernard Nickel, Mark Richard, Jonathan Schaffer, Ted Sider, and Scott Sturgeon. Jim Pryor and Nico Silins gave me very helpful comments on the whole manuscript, as well as regular conversations about epistemology. Jeffrey King provided me with an extremely important suggestion about how to deal with some recalcitrant examples, as well as helpful discussion throughout the writing of this book. His contribution to my work culminated in a detailed commentary on Chapter 7, presented at the USC conference on Syntax and Semantics with Attitude in 2005. Stewart Cohen sent me extensive and helpful comments on a time slice of the paper that descended from the 2002 conference, which caused a number of important changes.

My greatest debts for comments are due to Brian Weatherson, Jim Joyce, Keith DeRose, John Hawthorne, and Timothy Williamson. Weatherson was present at several of the talks I have given on this material, and made points that significantly changed the direction of my thinking. Jim Joyce not only provided me with the aforementioned education on formal epistemology, but was a tireless interlocutor and commentator on this work during my time at Michigan. I have spoken with DeRose for years about the topics of this book, and he has proven to be an extraordinarily helpful e-mail correspondent. Furthermore, he provided me with extensive comments on the penultimate version. Hawthorne and I started talking intensively about these topics around the year 2001, and were presenting defenses of interest-relativism about knowledge at the same conferences. We continued our conversations over many years, and in the summer of 2004 I had the privilege of joining him as a colleague at Rutgers. I spent the academic year 2004–5 writing up this material into book form. The whole process was made much easier by the fact that I could go into the department, relate my ideas to Hawthorne, and receive his incredibly incisive feedback.

By far my largest debt is to Timothy Williamson. I have discussed every aspect of this book with Williamson, and he has given me extensive comments at each stage of the project, from the very beginning to the very end (culminating in several three-hour phone conversations giving me page-by-page comments on the whole manuscript). Though he does not agree with my views, he was invaluable in helping me formulate the best versions of them. I have removed citations to discussion with him, since I would have had to acknowledge his influence on every page.

Peter Momtchiloff is a terrific editor for a high-maintenance author such as me. He has been responsive and encouraging, as has his staff at Oxford University Press. The philosophy departments at the University of Michigan and Rutgers are terrific environments to produce good work, and I am very grateful to my colleagues at both institutions (also for the research time these institutions provided). Thanks also to New College, Oxford, and the Research School of Social Science at Australian National University for visiting fellowships, during which some of this project was completed.

My wife Njeri feels guilty for not having read this book. But without the love and comfort she has provided over the last eleven years, neither this book nor much of anything positive in my life would have been possible. My wife and I both have busy careers; my mother helped at making the practical aspects of our lives manageable. Throughout the writing of this manuscript, I was traveling back and forth to Syracuse, New York, sometimes every week, to stay with my ill father Manfred, who passed away in September 2004. We talked regularly about the issues in this book, and I am sure the fact that he took the conclusions of this book as obvious had some effect on my ability to overcome the 'incredulous-stare' objection. I miss the robustness of his faith that abstract philosophy has some bearing on the human condition, and I miss him too. This book is dedicated to his memory.

CONTENTS

Introduction

A central part of epistemology, as traditionally conceived, consists of the study of the factors in virtue of which someone's true belief is an instance of knowledge. The factors that have been proposed in epistemology are typically ones that are *truth-conducive*, in the sense that their existence makes the belief more likely to be true, either objectively or from the point of view of the subject. Much of epistemology has been devoted to debates between advocates of differing truth-conducive factors. For example, epistemic internalists have argued that the additional truth-conducive factors are other beliefs. Epistemic externalists have argued that the relevant truth-conducive factors include the fact that the belief is the product of a reliable belief-forming mechanism. All of these debates are between theorists who hold that only truth-conducive factors are relevant to the question of what makes it the case that someone's true belief is an instance of knowledge.

It is no surprise that epistemologists have widely shared the assumption that the additional factors that make a true belief into knowledge are uniformly truth conducive (either objectively or from the point of view of the subject). The differences between true belief and knowledge are matters that fall within the purview of theoretical rationality, which many philosophers hold to be guided solely by the normative purpose of discovering the truth. My purpose in this book is to challenge this conception of knowledge. I will argue that the factors that make true belief into knowledge include elements from practical rationality. One consequence of my arguments is that the distinction between practical and theoretical rationality is less clear than one might wish.

Someone's practical investment in the truth or falsity of her belief is completely irrelevant to truth conduciveness in any sense. From the traditional perspective, then, when someone has a true belief, whether that belief is genuine knowledge is independent of *the costs of being wrong*. My aim is to provide a systematic case against this thesis. I join several recent authors in arguing that our *practical interests* have epistemic significance.[1] There are cases in which two people are similarly situated, but one has knowledge, whereas the other does not, because one has greater practical investment in the truth or falsity of her beliefs. What makes true belief into knowledge is not entirely an epistemic matter.

This conclusion is bound to sound somewhat paradoxical, because there are two senses in which epistemologists are prone to use the term 'epistemic'. On one use of 'epistemic', it denotes truth-conducive factors, in the broad sense in which I have sketched above. On the other understanding of 'epistemic', it has to do with factors relevant to whether a true belief is knowledge. The thesis of this book is that, contrary to epistemological orthodoxy, these two usages of the term do not coincide. Using 'epistemic' in the first of these ways, then, the thesis of the book is that what makes true belief into knowledge is not entirely an epistemic matter.

The book is short, because many of the elements of my argument have already been set in place by those with different goals. In particular, *contextualists* about knowledge ascriptions have discovered many of the examples that suggest that whether

[1] See Fantl and McGrath (2002) and Hawthorne (2004: ch. 4).

a true belief is knowledge depends not just upon truth-conducive features of a situation, but on what is practically at stake.[2] However, contextualists generally share the widely held assumption that knowledge is not a matter of practical interests. So they have used these examples, together with the assumption, to argue for the thesis that a predicate such as 'knows that penguins waddle' denotes different knowledge properties on different occasions of use. Each of the resulting semantic contents is a property, possession of which does not depend upon practical interests. But which such property is denoted by a knowledge-attributing predicate depends upon practical factors, such as how much is at stake. In this way, the contextualist can explain the examples without violating the commonly shared assumption that knowledge is not a matter of practical interests.

Contextualists have generally been interested in establishing the context-sensitivity of knowledge ascriptions in order to use the insight in the resolution of various traditional philosophical problems, such as explaining away the persuasive force of skeptical arguments. They have tended not to consider explicitly the assumption that what makes true belief into knowledge is purely a matter of truth-conducive factors, in the sense described above. But the interest of the examples they have employed to argue for the context-sensitivity of knowledge ascriptions is precisely that, when taken at face value, they do suggest the falsity of this assumption. Once we see that knowledge ascriptions are not context-sensitive in any distinctively epistemological way, we are led by such examples to reject the common assumption that knowledge (to put it tendentiously) is a purely epistemic notion.

Here are the examples I will focus upon; they have largely been made famous by others.

Low Stakes. Hannah and her wife Sarah are driving home on a Friday afternoon. They plan to stop at the bank on the way

[2] In particular, most of the examples have been discovered by Stewart Cohen and Keith DeRose.

home to deposit their paychecks. It is not important that they do so, as they have no impending bills. But as they drive past the bank, they notice that the lines inside are very long, as they often are on Friday afternoons. Realizing that it isn't very important that their paychecks are deposited right away, Hannah says, 'I know the bank will be open tomorrow, since I was there just two weeks ago on Saturday morning. So we can deposit our paychecks tomorrow morning.'

High Stakes. Hannah and her wife Sarah are driving home on a Friday afternoon. They plan to stop at the bank on the way home to deposit their paychecks. Since they have an impending bill coming due, and very little in their account, it is very important that they deposit their paychecks by Saturday. Hannah notes that she was at the bank two weeks before on a Saturday morning, and it was open. But, as Sarah points out, banks do change their hours. Hannah says, 'I guess you're right. I don't know that the bank will be open tomorrow.'

Low Attributor–High Subject Stakes. Hannah and her wife Sarah are driving home on a Friday afternoon. They plan to stop at the bank on the way home to deposit their paychecks. Since they have an impending bill coming due, and very little in their account, it is very important that they deposit their paychecks by Saturday. Two weeks earlier, on a Saturday, Hannah went to the bank, where Jill saw her. Sarah points out to Hannah that banks do change their hours. Hannah utters, 'That's a good point. I guess I don't really know that the bank will be open on Saturday.' Coincidentally, Jill is thinking of going to the bank on Saturday, just for fun, to see if she meets Hannah there. Nothing is at stake for Jill, and she knows nothing of Hannah's situation. Wondering whether Hannah will be there, Jill utters to a friend, 'Well, Hannah was at the bank two weeks ago on a Saturday. So she knows the bank will be open on Saturday.'

Ignorant High Stakes. Hannah and her wife Sarah are driving home on a Friday afternoon. They plan to stop at the bank on the way home to deposit their paychecks. Since they have an impending bill coming due, and very little in their account, it is very important that they deposit their paychecks by Saturday. But neither Hannah nor Sarah is aware of the impending bill, nor of the paucity of available funds. Looking at the lines, Hannah says to Sarah, 'I know the bank will be open tomorrow, since I was there just two weeks ago on Saturday morning. So we can deposit our paychecks tomorrow morning.'

High Attributor–Low Subject Stakes. Hannah and her wife Sarah are driving home on a Friday afternoon. They plan to stop at the bank on the way home to deposit their paychecks. Since they have an impending bill coming due, and very little in their account, it is very important that they deposit their paychecks by Saturday. Hannah calls up Bill on her cell phone, and asks Bill whether the bank will be open on Saturday. Bill replies by telling Hannah, 'Well, I was there two weeks ago on a Saturday, and it was open.' After reporting the discussion to Sarah, Hannah concludes that, since banks do occasionally change their hours, 'Bill doesn't really know that the bank will be open on Saturday'.

Suppose that, in all five situations, the bank will be open on Saturday. Here, I take it, are the intuitive reactions we have about these cases. In Low Stakes, our reaction is that Hannah is right; her utterance of 'I know the bank will be open' is true. In High Stakes, our reaction is that Hannah is also right. Her utterance of 'I don't know that the bank will be open' is true. In Low Attributor–High Subject Stakes, our intuition is that Jill's utterance of 'she knows the bank will be open on Saturday' is false. In Ignorant High Stakes, our reaction is that Hannah's utterance of 'I know the bank will be open tomorrow' is false. In High Attributor–Low Subject Stakes, our reaction is that Hannah's utterance of 'Bill doesn't really know that the bank will be open on Saturday' is true.

The *practical facts* about a situation are facts about the costs of being right or wrong about one's beliefs. All five cases involve people with the same non-practical basis for the belief the bank will be open the next morning (in the first four, Hannah, and in the fifth, Bill). But the facts as to whether the relevant attributor can truly ascribe the predicate 'knows that the bank will be open' to the relevant subject vary. Furthermore, the facts vary in accord with the *importance* to some person—either the knowledge attributor or the putative knower—of the bank's being open. This provides a prima facie case for the thesis that knowledge is not just a matter of non-practical facts, but is also a matter of *how much is at stake.*

I will call the thesis that knowledge does not depend upon practical facts *intellectualism.*[3] Intellectualism is a wide orthodoxy. So conservatism demands the exploration of alternative paths. For example, one might attempt to explain away the force of the intuitions behind these scenarios, by arguing that, when someone recognizes that the costs of being wrong are particularly high, his or her confidence is shaken. The result of having one's confidence shaken is either to reduce one's degree of belief below the threshold required for knowledge or to defeat the evidence one has for one's belief in some other manner. This explanation provides an elegant account of the second scenario, where Hannah's awareness of the costs of being wrong undermines her confidence in her belief.[4]

However, this line of defense falters when one considers Ignorant High Stakes. In this case, Hannah's confidence that the bank will be open is not shaken, because she is ignorant of the potential costs of not depositing her check. So the defender

---

[3] Thanks to Earl Conee for suggesting this term.

[4] Jon Kvanvig (on the blog Certain Doubts) suggested this as an account of these sorts of cases.

of this line of defense would have to adopt the position that Hannah does not know that the bank will be open in the second scenario, but *does* know that the bank will be open in the fourth scenario. And this is an odd position. After all, Hannah is more knowledgeable about her situation in the second scenario than she is in the fourth scenario. It does not seem correct that adding a little ignorance increases knowledge. In short, if Hannah does not know in the second scenario, it seems she also does not know in the fourth scenario. If so, then appealing to loss of confidence does not help in evading the consequence that practical interests can have epistemic consequences.

This line of defense also does not account for our intuitions concerning High Attributor–Low Subject Stakes. We may suppose that Bill's confidence that the bank will be open is not affected by Hannah and Sarah's situation. So the account does not provide an explanation of our intuition that Hannah and Sarah are correct to deny knowledge to Bill. So some other explanation is required.

Another strategy that proponents of intellectualism commonly appeal to in the face of these examples is to argue that in certain cases our responses are sensitive not to whether the subject knows, but to whether the subject *knows* that she knows. According to advocates of this strategy, Hannah knows that the bank will be open in Low Stakes, High Stakes, and Ignorant High Stakes, and Bill knows that the bank will be open in High Attributor–Low Subject Stakes. Our judgments to the contrary in the latter three cases are to be explained by the fact that the relevant subjects do not *know that they know* in any of these cases. According to this line of reasoning, knowing that one knows that *p* requires having more evidence for *p* than knowing that *p*. When we are aware that the stakes are particularly high for a subject, we tend to require not just that the subject knows the propositions upon which she bases her actions, but that she knows that she knows those propositions. Our awareness of the raised stakes for Hannah in High Stakes leads us to think that she needs to know that she knows that the bank will be open, and not merely know that the bank will be open. Since she does not face a potentially hazardous predicament in Low Stakes, we are not led to make the error of thinking that she does not know that the bank will be open.

I am inclined to reject the KK thesis that knowing that *p* entails knowing that one knows that *p*. But I have difficulty seeing how the falsity of that thesis can be brought to bear to explain away these intuitions. First, the proponent of this way of rejecting our intuitions about these cases must explain why the fact that an agent does not know that she knows that *p* would lead us to deny that the agent knows that *p*. This requires an entirely independent explanation. Secondly, the proponent of this response must give some good reason to believe that in each case in which someone in a 'low-stakes' situation (such as Hannah in Low Stakes) seems to know that *p*, whereas someone with comparable evidence in a 'high-stakes' situation does not seem to know that *p*, the person in the low-stakes situation does not know that she knows that *p*.

I am skeptical that a good justification for the second claim can be provided. Most ordinary assertions of knowledge are made on such a basis that we can envisage someone in a higher-stakes situation (often a much higher-stakes situation), whom we would not think of as possessing that knowledge, given similar evidence. The proponent of this response would have to argue that, in all such cases, the person in the low-stakes situation knows that *p*, but does not know that she knows that *p*. This leads to widespread failure of knowledge of knowledge. It is one thing to deny that knowledge entails knowing that one knows, but it is quite another to license such a wholesale denial of knowledge of knowledge.[5]

---

[5] Here is another point against the knowledge of knowledge maneuver, due to unpublished work by Kripke. Suppose that Hannah, in the low-stakes bank case, knows that the bank will be open. Suppose Bill has the same evidence as

A third reaction one might have when confronted by these cases is to explain them away as various types of *framing effects*, of the sort familiar from recent psychological studies of rationality. It has been established that our judgments about the rationality of various inferences are highly dependent upon idiosyncratic facts about how the background situation is described. It would be unwise to put very much weight upon this evidence in claims about the nature of rationality. Similarly, one might think that the intuitions we have in the above cases are also due to psychological framing effects. If so, they are unlikely to be helpful in inquiry into the nature of the knowledge relation.

However, the above cases reveal intuitions that are not analogous to the framing effects we see in ordinary speakers' judgments about rationality. The latter sort of judgment does not follow a discernible pattern that reflects any plausible general claim about rationality. In contrast, the intuitions we have in the above cases are just the intuitions we would expect to have, if certain antecedently plausible conceptual connections between knowledge and practical reasoning were true. As other anti-intellectuals have argued (Fantl and McGrath 2002, and especially Hawthorne 2004), it is immensely plausible to take knowledge to be constitutively connected to action, in the sense that *one should act only on what one knows*.[6] For various theoretical reasons, this

Hannah, and is also in a low-stakes situation. Then Bill can felicitously and truly utter the sentence 'I know that Hannah knows that the bank will be open'. It seems bizarre to hold, as the advocate of this maneuver must, that Bill knows that Hannah knows that the bank will be open, but Hannah does not know that Hannah knows that the bank will be open, despite the fact that they have the same evidence that the bank will be open.

[6] John Hawthorne (2004: 30) puts the principle as 'one ought only to use that which one knows as a premise in one's deliberations', which is a good way to elucidate the relevant sense of 'act on'. Hawthorne writes, concerning this principle: 'There are complications that call for *ceteris paribus* style qualifications. In a situation where I have no clue what is going on, I may take certain things for granted in order to prevent paralysis, especially when I need to act

immensely plausible claim has not traditionally been accepted by those studying practical reasoning. But rejecting this claim devalues the role of knowledge in our ordinary conceptual scheme.

A standard use of knowledge attributions is to justify action. When I am asked why I went to the store on the left, rather than the store on the right, I will respond by saying that I knew that the store on the left had the newspaper I wanted, but I did not know whether the store on the right did. When my wife asks me why I turned left rather than going straight, I reply that I knew that it was the shortest direction to the restaurant. When it turns out that it was not a way to go to the restaurant at all, my wife will point out that I only *believed* that it was the shortest way to the restaurant. To say that an action is only based on a belief is to criticize that action for not living up to an expected norm; to say that an action is based on knowledge is to declare that the action has met the expected norm.

The fact that knowledge is thus connected to action is obscured by several points. First, *assertion* is also conceptually connected to knowledge; asserting that p implicates that one knows that p. So, in defending an action based upon one's knowledge that p, it is enough simply to assert that p. Secondly, in certain special circumstances, we do occasionally act on our knowledge that there is a *chance* that p, rather than our knowledge that p.[7] For example, there are lotteries in which it is rational for me to buy a ticket, even though I do not know that I will win; when pressed to defend my purchase, I will respond that there is a chance I will win. But this is just to say that there are certain types of actions that I perform on the basis of beliefs about chances. In order for these actions to be acceptable, such beliefs must still constitute knowledge.

---

quickly.' But *ceteris paribus* style qualifications are needed only insofar as they are needed in all normative claims. A similar point holds for the knowledge rule for assertion, discussed below.

[7] Thanks to Jim Pryor for discussion here.

The intuitions we have in the above cases are best explained by appeal to our commitment to the principle that one should act only upon what one knows. For example, in High Stakes, we think it is mistaken for Hannah to act on her belief that the bank will be open on Saturday, and wait until Saturday to go there. The obvious reason why Hannah should not wait until Saturday to go to the bank is that she does not know that the bank will be open. The same is true for Ignorant High Stakes. Indeed, the intuitions in virtually all of the above cases are exactly the ones we would expect to have if it is true that knowledge is connected to action in the above sense.[8] The intuitions therefore provide powerful intuitive evidence for an antecedently plausible principle concerning the relation between knowledge and action.

It is odd to assert instances of the schema 'P, but I don't know that P' (Moore's Paradox). The oddity of asserting instances of Moore's Paradox is often taken to be strong evidence for the intuitive connection between assertion and knowledge (e.g. Williamson 2000: 253–5), that *one ought only to assert what one knows*. It is highly unlikely that the oddity of Moore's Paradox is due to a psychological framing effect. For a similar reason, the reactions we have to virtually all of the cases I have discussed are not random noise. They are rather natural reflections of the conceptual connections between knowledge and action, of our intuitive adherence to the principle that one should act only upon what one knows.

So there is no easy intellectualist strategy for explaining away the intuitions. This leaves the intellectual with the following quandary. If the thesis that one's knowledge of one of one's true beliefs depends only upon non-practical facts is correct, then it cannot both be the case that (for example) Hannah

[8] I say 'virtually all the cases', because the one intuition that remains mysterious from this perspective is the intuition we have in High Attributor–Low Subject Stakes. It is fine for the person in Low Stakes to act on his or her belief that the bank will be open.

knows that the bank will be open in Low Stakes, and does not know that the bank is open in the other three relevant situations. For, by stipulation, the non-practical facts for Hannah are the same in all of these cases, and she even has the same degree of confidence in her belief (at least in Low Stakes and Ignorant High Stakes). So, either the thesis must be rejected, or some other natural assumption.

Here are the options available to one who wishes to preserve the independence of knowledge from practical facts:

(a) One can challenge the claim that these are the intuitions we have in these cases.

(b) One can reject the semantic significance of one of the intuitions. For example, one could deny semantic significance to the intuition that the proposition semantically expressed by Hannah's utterance in Low Stakes is true. Alternatively, one could deny semantic significance to the intuition that the proposition semantically expressed by Hannah's utterance in High Stakes is true (or reject the semantic significance of either of the intuitions in the other two cases).

(c) One can deny that the proposition expressed by Hannah's utterance in Low Stakes is really the denial of the proposition expressed by Hannah's utterance in High Stakes (and make similar maneuvers for the other two cases).

Though I certainly do not take all of the intuitions we have in the above cases as indefeasible, I will not discuss except in passing the first of these options. The role of these intuitions is not akin to the role of observational data for a scientific theory. The intuitions are instead intended to reveal the powerful intuitive sway of the thesis that knowledge is the basis for action. Someone who denies that we have many of these intuitions is denying the pull of the link between knowledge to action. But the *value* of knowledge is explicable in part by its links to action; it is for this reason that skepticism threatens agency. Those who deny these intuitions are in effect maintaining that some other notion, such as appropriately confident belief, is intuitively the genuinely valuable one. It is because I find this reaction so implausible that I will not seriously consider rejecting these intuitions. Nevertheless, while my central interest is to evaluate accounts that make as much sense of these intuitions as possible, the central claims of this book hold, even if some of the above intuitions are less robust than others. I will leave it to the reader to decide which arguments in the book are strengthened or weakened by her particular pattern of intuitions.

As far as the second of these options is concerned, the most obvious way to develop it is to appeal to a certain view about the relation between semantics and pragmatics. According to this view, our intuitions about what is said by utterances of sentences are not in general reliable guides to the semantic contents of sentences in context, even relative to perfectly clear hypothetical circumstances like the ones described above. On this view, our intuitions about what is said by a sentence are often influenced by pragmatic, post-semantic content conveyed by the act of asserting that sentence.

For example, one might argue that we are wrong to think that Hannah's utterance in Low Stakes expresses a true proposition, because 'know' expresses a relation that holds between a person and only a very few select propositions, those for which (say) she has deductive valid arguments from a priori premises. But knowledge ascriptions may pragmatically convey that the subject stands in some epistemically looser relation with the proposition. One could then 'explain' the mistaken intuition on the hypothesis that we often confuse what an assertion of a sentence pragmatically conveys with the semantic content of that sentence relative to a context.

Giving pragmatic explanations of apparently semantic intuitions is a standard maneuver in philosophy. While this strategy is certainly occasionally called for, it must be applied with great circumspection. For example, DeRose (1999) considers a crazed theorist who defends the view that 'bachelor' just expresses the property of being a man. This theorist holds that the intuition that 'is a bachelor' cannot be truly predicated of a married man has no semantic significance; it is due rather to (say) pragmatic felicity conditions governing the use of the term 'bachelor'. DeRose's point in considering such examples is that the tendency philosophers have to give pragmatic rather than semantic explanations of apparently semantic intuitions threatens to undermine the whole enterprise of giving semantic explanations. As he writes (1999: 198), concerning pragmatic explanations of speakers' apparently semantic intuitions about the cases that motivate his favored view:

It's an instance of a general scheme that, if allowed, could be used to far too easily explain away the counterexamples marshaled against any theory about the truth-conditions of sentence forms in natural language. Whenever you face an apparent counterexample—where your theory says that what seems false is true, or when it says that what seems true is false—you can very easily just ascribe the apparent truth (falsehood) to the warranted (unwarranted) assertability of the sentence in the circumstances problematic to your theory. If we allow such maneuvers, we'll completely lose our ability to profitably test theories against examples.

By undermining the data for semantic theory, this kind of strategy threatens to undermine the semantic project.

Of course, there are cases in which it is legitimate to provide pragmatic explanations of apparent semantic intuitions. Again, to borrow an example from DeRose (1999: 196 ff.), if someone clearly knows that p, it seems extremely odd to say that p is epistemically possible for that person. But there is a clear explanation from Gricean principles for the oddity in question. There is a general conversational principle to the effect that one should always assert the most informative proposition one is in a position to assert. If x asserts 'It is possible that p', then x implicates, via this maxim, 'I do not know that p'. Our sense that such an assertion is odd, or seems false, is due to the fact that x is implicating something known to be false. The problem with many pragmatic explanations of apparently semantic intuitions is that there is no such clear explanation from general conversational principles.

Denying the semantic significance of apparently semantic intuitions is a significant cost, one that we should be reluctant to bear in the absence of a clear explanation of these intuitions from general conversational principles. Since I am not aware of such an explanation, I think that the most fruitful way to pursue preserving intellectualism is by appeal to the third option. And this leads us to the thesis of contextualism.

I

Contextualism

Contextualism is the semantic thesis that knowledge ascriptions, instances of 'x knows that p', are context-sensitive in a distinctively epistemological way. That is, predicates such as 'knows that the bank on the Corner of 96th and Broadway in New York City will be open on Saturday, September 11, 2004', or 'knows that Bill Clinton was president of the United States of America in 1999', express different properties relative to different contexts, despite their apparent lack of context-sensitive vocabulary.

A sentence is context-sensitive if and only if it expresses different propositions relative to different contexts of use. The contextualist claim is that, in addition to typical context-sensitivity (such as tense and uncontroversial context-sensitive constructions), knowledge ascriptions have an additional kind of context-sensitivity. The bare thesis of contextualism leaves open various ways to implement it. As we will see below, most contextualists have claimed that 'know' is, like 'I', 'here', and 'now', an indexical expression. But one might also argue that the context-sensitivity of knowledge ascriptions is due to the fact that the verb 'know' is associated with an additional position for epistemic standards, which are supplied contextually. On this way of construing contextualism, while the word 'know' itself is not context-sensitive, predicates that are instances of the schema 'knows that *p'* are context-sensitive, since they are really of the form 'knows that *p* relative to standards *s'*, where *s* receives a value from context (cf. Ludlow 2005). On yet another way of implementing contextualism, advocated by Jonathan Schaffer (2004), the word 'know' is associated with an additional position for what he calls a *contrast proposition*. On all of these views, instances of the schema 'knows that *p'* are context-sensitive in a distinctively epistemological way. According to the proponents of these views, the semantic context-sensitivity of an instance of 'knows that *p'* goes beyond the resolution of tense and other uncontroversial context-sensitive expressions occurring in the embedded sentence.

Contextualism is not simply silent on how it is to be semantically implemented; it is also silent on all epistemological matters. Contextualism is not a theory of knowledge, or even of 'knowledge', any more than the claim that the word 'dog' is context-sensitive is a theory of dogs or even of 'dog'. Since the contextualist thesis is simply that knowledge ascriptions are context-sensitive in a distinctively epistemological manner, it is consistent with a wide variety of epistemological views. If one implements contextualism semantically as the thesis that the term 'know' is an indexical expression that expresses different knowledge relations relative to different contexts of use, the resulting thesis is consistent with many views of the nature of the denoted knowledge relations.

Contextualism was originally advanced both as an interpretation (Goldman 1976: 776–7) and as an improvement (Stine 1976) of Dretske's *Relevant Alternatives Theory* (Dretske 1970). According to Relevant Alternatives Theory (henceforth RAT), knowing a true proposition one believes at a time requires being able to rule out relevant alternatives to that proposition at that time. On Dretske's view, looking at a zebra in a zoo, I know that it is a zebra. I know that what I am looking at is a zebra, because, in a typical visit to the zoo, the proposition that (as it might be) what I am looking at is a cleverly painted mule is not a relevant alternative to the proposition that it is a zebra. So I do not need to rule out the proposition that the animal I am looking at is a cleverly painted mule in order to know that what I am looking at is a zebra.

However, according to Dretske, I do not know that the animal I am looking at is not a cleverly painted mule. The proposition that the animal I am looking at *is* a cleverly painted mule is a relevant alternative to the proposition that the animal I am looking at is not a cleverly painted mule. According to Dretske, I have no special evidence against the proposition that the animal I am looking at is a cleverly painted mule, since my visual evidence is compatible with this possibility. So I cannot rule out a relevant alternative to the proposition that the animal I am looking at is not a cleverly painted mule. So I do not know that the animal I am looking at is not a cleverly painted mule, even though I know something that directly entails it—namely, that the animal is a zebra.

There are many worries with RAT. First, it is not clear what it is to rule out an alternative. Secondly, it is not clear how to draw the distinction between relevant and irrelevant alternatives. But perhaps the most worrying consequence is that it results in a straightforward failure of *single-premise epistemic closure*.[1] To a first approximation, single-premise epistemic closure is the thesis that, if someone knows the conjunction that p and that the

---

[1] I am here distinguishing single-premise epistemic closure from multi-premise closure. To a first approximation, multi-premise closure is that if one knows that $p_1 \ldots p_n$, and simultaneously knows that $p_1 \ldots p_n$ entail q, then one also knows that q. Both single-premise and multi-premise closure have an intuitive grounding in the claim that deduction is a way of gaining knowledge (see Williamson 2000: 117–18). But there are theoretical objections to multi-premise epistemic closure that are not objections to single-premise epistemic closure. For example, since a conjunction is in general less probable than any of its conjuncts, deducing a conjunction from multiple premises does not preserve a high probability attaching to each individual premise. This worry does not arise for single-premise epistemic closure.

proposition that p entails the proposition that q, then that person knows that q. According to the advocate of RAT, I know that what I am looking at is a zebra, but I do not know that it is not a cleverly painted mule, even though I am fully aware that what I know entails what I supposedly do not know. Similarly, according to the advocate of RAT, I know that I have hands, and that having hands entails that I am not a handless brain in a vat, but I do not know that I am not a handless brain in a vat. I know that I have hands, since it is not a relevant alternative to my having hands that I am a handless brain in a vat. So I do not need to rule out the possibility that I am a handless brain in a vat in order to know that I have hands. But the proposition that I am a handless brain in a vat is an alternative to the possibility that I am not a handless brain in a vat. Since, according to the advocate of RAT, I cannot rule that proposition out, I do not know that I am not a handless brain in a vat. So I know that I have hands, and I know that having hands entails not being a handless brain in a vat, but I do not know, and am not even in a position to know, that I am not a handless brain in a vat.

The relevant alternative theorist's rejection of single-premise epistemic closure is a theoretical cost. But the cost can also be felt on the intuitive level. As Keith DeRose (1995: 27–9) has emphasized, utterances of constructions such as the following are particularly infelicitous:

(1) John knows that he has hands, but he does not know that he is not a handless brain in a vat.
(2) John knows that that is a zebra, but he does not know that that is not a painted mule.

But, if RAT is correct, utterances of (1) and (2) express true propositions. Since there is no other obvious source of their infelicity, RAT has inexplicably bad consequences.

A contextualist construal of RAT promises to overcome several problems with it. By adopting it, one can grant some legitimacy to the otherwise mysterious distinction between relevant and irrelevant alternatives. If someone utters 'Everything is put away', the domain of their use of 'everything' is determined by what objects the speaker has in mind. That is, the domain of a quantifier expression is determined by what is salient to its user, where salience is some psychological notion. If instances of 'know that p' are context-sensitive, then presumably their semantic values are determined by what possibilities their users have in mind—that is, what possibilities are salient to them. Thus, the mysterious distinction between relevant and irrelevant alternatives can be grounded in a psychological distinction between what is salient to a speaker versus what is not salient to a speaker, a distinction already independently required in the study of context-sensitivity.

What generally takes the place of discussions about how to make the distinction between relevant and irrelevant alternatives, in the contextualist literature, are discussions of when the context shifts to a higher-standards knowledge property (cf. DeRose 1995; Lewis 1996). There are problems with all extant proposals. But, since there is no good account of these matters for uncontroversial context-sensitive expressions, perhaps the contextualist is not in a worse situation than the rest of us. If the contextualist can show that the shifts she requires over a discourse for her explanations of the data from lower-standards knowledge properties to higher-standards knowledge properties occur in a similar pattern to shifts in content with other context-sensitive expressions (say, from one standard of tallness to another), she has fulfilled her obligations. This is a much easier task, on the face of it, than providing a principled distinction between relevant and irrelevant alternatives.

Another major benefit of construing RAT in contextualist terms is, as Gail Stine (1976) emphasizes in her pioneering article, that one can preserve epistemic closure, and explain the oddity of the discourses in (1) and (2). Suppose that what is salient to the speaker will remain in force across a discourse. So, in (1) and (2), the relevant alternatives salient to the user are the same for the first conjunct and the second conjunct. When we hold fixed the possibilities salient to a speaker across a discourse, and evaluate all uses of epistemic terms relative to that fixed set, then all the relevant alternatives for the proposition that the animal John is looking at is not a painted mule are relevant alternatives for the proposition that the animal John is looking at is a zebra. So, if John knows that the animal he is looking at is a zebra, then he has ruled out all salient alternatives, and hence ruled out all salient alternatives to the proposition that the animal he is looking at is not a painted mule (Stine 1976: sect 3).

Relative to a context in which an utterance of 'John knows that the animal he is looking at is a zebra' expresses a true proposition, so will an utterance of 'John knows that the animal he is looking at is not a painted mule'. But in another context, when the possibility that the animal he is looking at is a painted mule is salient, neither utterance would express a true proposition. Stine is therefore able to capture both the intuition that some utterances of 'John knows that the animal he is looking at is a zebra' express true propositions, and the intuition that some utterances of 'John does not know that the animal he is looking at is not a painted mule' express true propositions, even when there is no change in John's evidential state. She is furthermore able to capture these Dretskian intuitions without appeal to a mysterious distinction between relevant and irrelevant alternatives, and without rejecting single-premise epistemic closure. Finally, because of these improvements, she is able to explain the infelicity of utterances of (1) and (2).

So, contextualism was originally proposed as an improvement on RAT, one that promises to preserve single-premise epistemic closure, and explain the infelicity of utterances of (1) and (2). But one might equally well marry contextualism with any other epistemological view. For example, one might think that knowledge of a true proposition one believes is fundamentally a matter of the strength of one's evidence. In that case, one might take the different potential knowledge relations to vary according to how strong one's evidence must be in order to stand in that relation to a proposition (this is a view advocated by Stewart Cohen). The bare thesis of contextualism does not tell us which view of the different knowledge relations to adopt.

The bare thesis of contextualism is also silent on what facts about a context make it the case that a knowledge ascription has one content rather than another. It is consistent with the letter of contextualism, for example, to adopt the position that, in the epistemology classroom, the word 'know' denotes a relation that is less epistemically strict than the relation denoted by the word 'know' outside the epistemology classroom. However, if knowledge ascriptions are context-sensitive, then presumably the facts that explain what contents they possess, relative to different contexts, should not differ radically from the kinds of facts that account for the varying contents of uncontroversial context-sensitive expressions. So, while the bare thesis of contextualism is silent about what makes it the case that an instance of 'x knows that p' has one content rather than another, it is presumably constrained by empirical facts about context-sensitivity in natural language.

We have explored in some detail Stine's motivation for moving to a contextualist version of RAT. The contributions of Stewart Cohen and Keith DeRose have been to provide some additional motivations for moving from one's favored epistemological theories to contextualist versions of them. In particular, Cohen and DeRose have argued that contextualist versions of epistemological theories have the most promise in explaining the kinds of intuitions concerning the cases discussed in the Introduction, without violating intellectualism.

Suppose we add on to the bare contextualist thesis the following two claims:

Claim 1. Knowledge states are ordered according to epistemic 'strength'.[2] It is easier to be in some knowledge states than it is

---

[2] The ordering among knowledge states that involve the same content does not need to be a linear ordering. For example, some multi-grade adjectives may not impose a linear ordering on their domains.

to be in other knowledge states, even when the two know-ledge states involve 'knowledge' of the same proposition. That is, one must have more or better evidence to be in one of these knowledge states rather than the other, even when they in-volve the same proposition.

Claim 2. What determines the semantic value of instances of 'knows that *p*', relative to a context of use, is some collection of facts about the intentions and beliefs of the conversational participants in that context of use.

If we add these two claims to the bare thesis of contextualism, together with some plausible additional assumptions, we can go some way towards explaining the intuitions in the cases discussed in the Introduction.

Coupled with any number of standard approaches to know-ledge (relations), contextualism has no trouble with Low Stakes. Nothing is at stake for Hannah, and so the semantic value of her use of 'know that the bank will be open on Saturday', relative to the envisaged context of use, will be one that is true of her, given only a modicum of evidence. The contextualist who endorses these two theses also has no trouble with accounting for our intuitions about High Stakes. In this case, Hannah is aware of the importance of the check being deposited before Monday. So we may suppose that her mental states determine a 'higher-strength' epistemic property as the semantic value for 'know that the bank will be open on Saturday'. Hannah must therefore have a great deal of evidence that the bank will be open on the following day in order for the property expressed in that context by the predi-cate 'knows that the bank will be open on Saturday' to be true of her. Since she does not have enough evidence, that property is not true of her.

This contextualist position also accounts for our intuitions concerning High Attributor–Low Subject Stakes. According to the contextualist, the content of the sentence 'Bill knows that the bank will be open on Saturday' is determined by the epistemic situation in the context of its use. Since Hannah and Sarah are both aware of the importance of depositing the check, knowledge attributions made in the context of a discussion between them will require a higher epistemic position on the part of the putative knower (in this case, Bill). Since Bill's evidence is not strong enough, he does not satisfy the predicate 'knows that the bank will be open on Saturday', relative to the context of Hannah and Sarah's discussion.

The envisaged contextualist position is one that can respect the thesis that whether one of one's true beliefs constitutes knowledge is independent of practical facts. Consider a particular instance of the schema 'x knows that p'. What property is expressed by the relevant instance of 'knows that p', relative to a context of use, is a function in part of practical facts about the context of use. But whether someone who truly believes that p has the property in question depends only upon non-practical facts about p. So the contextualist dissolves the threat the above cases pose by arguing that Hannah's utterances in Low Stakes and High Stakes do not conflict, just as utterances of 'I am tired' and 'I am not tired' do not conflict, when uttered by different people.

In contrast to these elegant accounts of Low Stakes, High Stakes, and High Attributor–Low Subject Stakes, the contextualist does not have any clear account of our intuitions in Low Attributor–High Subject Stakes. In this case, Jill asserts 'Hannah knows that the bank is open on Saturday, since she was there two weeks ago'. But, unbeknownst to Jill, Hannah is in a high-stakes situation. Intuitively, what Jill says is false. But, since Jill is in a low-stakes situation, the semantic value of her use of 'knows that the bank is open on Saturday' should be a property that Hannah possesses in virtue of having been to the bank two weeks previously. So the contextualist appears to predict falsely that Jill's assertion is true.

Adopting the 'confidence-shaking' maneuver discussed in the Introduction would also not aid the contextualist here. For we can envisage a case that stands to Low Attributor–High Subject Stakes as Ignorant High Stakes stands to High Stakes. That is, we can envisage a case in which Hannah and Sarah have a bill coming due, but are not aware of this fact, and so are very confident that they know that the bank will be open. Still, given what is at stake for Hannah if she is wrong, it seems that Jill's utterance of 'Hannah knows that the bank will be open' is false, since Hannah's evidence is not sufficient. Since (as in Ignorant High Stakes) Hannah is unaware of these costs, her confidence has not been shaken. Still, Jill's assertion is false, and contextualism has no account of its falsehood.

Furthermore, a contextualist who endorses the second claim, that the semantic content of instances of 'know that p' relative to a context is determined by the intentions of participants in that context, delivers the wrong account for Ignorant High Stakes. In that case, neither Hannah nor Sarah is aware of the costs of being wrong. Indeed, Hannah's referential intentions are the very same as they are in Low Stakes. So, if the facts that fix the semantic content of epistemic terms are determined by Hannah's (or even Hannah and Sarah's) intentions, then the content of Hannah's assertion will be the same as it is in Low Stakes. So, if something like the second claim is correct, contextualism predicts that Low Stakes and Ignorant High Stakes should be intuitively on a par, which of course they are not.

On a standard account of context-sensitive expressions, their semantic contents, relative to a context, are determined by facts about the intentions of the speaker using that expression. On this account, the reason that a use of (for example) 'that cat' refers to a particular cat is because of the linguistic meaning of 'that cat', together with the referential intentions of the user of that expression on that occasion. Call the view that all context-sensitive expressions behave in this manner the *intention-based* view of context-sensitive expressions. If this view is correct, then contextualism delivers the wrong result about Ignorant High Stakes, since the contextualist would then be committed to Claim 2.[3]

If, however, the contextualist about knowledge ascriptions can appeal to facts other than speaker intentions to fix the semantic content of knowledge ascriptions, she could potentially deliver a more satisfactory account of our intuitions about Ignorant High Stakes. In particular, to deliver results that accord with our intuitions about this case, she would have to argue that the *actual costs* that Hannah would incur in Ignorant High Stakes are semantically relevant. That is, it must turn out that the fact that there is a greater cost to Hannah's being wrong affects the semantic content of some of her statements, even when neither she, nor any other conversational participant, is aware of it. So the contextualist could accommodate Ignorant High Stakes, but only at the cost of advancing a rather dramatic claim about the potential semantic effects of non-psychological facts about extralinguistic context. Like other dramatic claims, this one carries with it additional costs.[4]

[3] Some theorists believe that there are some indexicals that have the semantic values they do independently of the intentions of their users. But even those who accept the existence of such a class agree that the list is very small, perhaps restricted to 'I', 'yesterday', 'tomorrow', and a few other terms. Even 'here' and 'now' are not automatic indexicals, since the spatial range of an occurrence of 'here' and the temporal range of an occurrence of 'now' are determined by a speaker's intentions. Other theorists (most recently and dramatically Gauker 2003) argue for the more revisionary thesis that non-mental facts do the reference-fixing work in a broad range of cases.

[4] Here is one. A version of contextualism that allows the subject's interests at the time of knowing to determine the semantic content of instances of 'know that *p*' faces some serious independent worries stemming from future tense attributions of knowledge, such as 'Hannah will know on Friday that the bank is open on Saturday'. Consider this sentence, as uttered on Tuesday, when Hannah's practical situation on Friday is not yet determined. Given that Hannah's practical situation on Friday is not yet determined, the semantic content of the predicate 'knows that the bank will be open on Saturday', as used on Tuesday, is also not yet determined. It is one thing to say that the *truth value* of future tensed

However, given many contextualists' broader epistemological goals, the contextualist generally accepts Claim 2, together with its consequences. As we have already seen, one of the benefits of a contextualist account of RAT is that it can appeal to the unquestionably robust psychological notion of salience to ground the otherwise mysterious distinction between relevant and irrelevant alternatives. If a contextualist abandons Claim 2, she therefore abandons one of the motivations for moving to a contextualist version of RAT.[5]

More importantly, the resulting potential shortcomings with Ignorant High Stakes can in fact be turned to the contextualist's advantage. Let BAD SITUATION be a situation in which I am having the experiences I am now having, but they are not veridical (perhaps because I am a brain in a vat not experiencing a veridical hallucination). Here is one standard formulation of a skeptical argument:

> *Premise 1.* I am not in a position to know that I am not in BAD SITUATION.
> *Premise 2.* I know that the proposition I am now facing a computer screen entails that I am not in BAD SITUATION.
> *Premise 3.* If I know that p, and I know that p entails q, then I am in a position to know that q.
> *Conclusion.* I do not know that I am facing a computer screen now.

statements is not yet determined when the future is metaphysically open. But it is vastly more implausible that the *semantic content* of an utterance such as this is not yet determined when the future is metaphysically open. But that is a consequence of the envisaged version of contextualism.

[5] Heller (1999) seems to advocate abandoning Claim 2, at least if salience to the conversational participants is the psychological feature that determines the semantic content of knowledge claims. I do not read DeRose (2004) as rejecting Claim 2, since his target there is the more restrictive claim that it is only the *speaker*'s intentions that do the semantic work.

The conclusion follows from the first three premises. So this argument is certainly valid, and it appears to have no easily disputable premise. However, if skeptical arguments are sound, then it appears that they undermine ordinary claims to know.

The standard contextualist's reaction to skeptical arguments is to try to explain away the threat posed by skeptical arguments to the truth of ordinary knowledge ascriptions. The standard contextualist does so, while accommodating the force of the skeptical argument. The idea behind the strategy is to grant that the propositions expressed by Premises 1–3 constitute a sound argument for the proposition expressed by the conclusion, whenever skeptical scenarios (bad situations) are salient. Relative to a context in which a bad situation is salient, the semantic value of instances of 'know that I am facing a computer screen now' is a property that I do not have (since I require much more than perceptual evidence to possess it). Consideration of such situations 'destroys knowledge'. But, according to the contextualist, this does not threaten ordinary knowledge ascriptions, ones made in contexts in which skeptical scenarios are not salient. Relative to a context in which no bad situations are salient, and all I want to do is check my e-mail, I can truly assert 'I know that I am facing a computer screen now', since, relative to such a context, the property expressed by the predicate 'know that I am facing a computer screen now' is one that I possess. Relative to such a context, I also am in a position to know that I have the property therein expressed by 'know that I am not in BAD SITUATION'. So, whenever skepticism is entertained, the sentences that form classical skeptical arguments (according to most contextualists) express sound arguments, since entertaining skepticism has the function of raising bad situations to salience. But skeptical arguments do not undermine ordinary knowledge ascriptions, since ordinary knowledge claims are made in contexts in which bad situations are not salient.

Of course, skeptics do take skeptical arguments to undermine ordinary knowledge ascriptions. According to the contextualist, the reason that skeptics take skeptical arguments to undermine normal knowledge attributions is because they make a certain type of semantic confusion. The confusion involves what John Hawthorne (2004: 107 ff.) has aptly named *semantic blindness*.

The thesis of semantic blindness is, as Hawthorne (2004) puts it, that 'There is a real sense in which users of the word "know" are blind to the semantic workings of their language'. In particular, we do not recognize the special kind of context-sensitivity of knowledge ascriptions. As a consequence, we tend to import facts about our own context into the interpretation of other discourses that involve knowledge ascriptions. The skeptic's error is to import facts about her own context into the interpretation of ordinary knowledge ascriptions, thereby coming to the conclusion that ordinary knowledge attributions have the same truth value as they would have, if uttered in the skeptic's context. This putative feature of language-users explains the skeptic's fallacy. By appealing to semantic blindness, the contextualist seeks to accommodate the force of skeptical arguments, while divesting them of the threat they pose to ordinary epistemic practice.[6]

Since semantic blindness is key to a certain contextualist explanation of our tendency to take skeptical arguments to undermine the truth of ordinary knowledge claims, those who seek to provide such an explanation should argue that our intuitions about Ignorant High Stakes are similarly distorted. This would provide an 'ordinary language' analogue to the mistake we allegedly make when contemplating the devastating epistemological consequences of skepticism. Since Claim 2 is crucial to one of the explanatory benefits of contextualism,

---

[6] The contextualist strategy in epistemology is thus similar to the contextualist strategy in addressing the sorites paradox—namely, to explain the force of the argument, while removing its most problematic consequences.

abandoning it is therefore not in the best interests of the advocate of contextualism.

As we have seen, contextualism is a weak epistemological thesis, but a strong semantic thesis. The strong semantic thesis is that epistemic terms are semantically context-sensitive. The contextualist has a good amount of motivation for her semantic thesis. First, there are the theoretical benefits. These include preserving single-premise epistemic closure, and providing a non-skeptical explanation of our tendency to take skeptical hypotheses as undermining ordinary knowledge claims. Secondly, there are intuitive benefits, such as providing an explanation for the infelicity of utterances of (1) and (2), and proving an explanation of our intuitions about many of the cases discussed in the Introduction. Nevertheless, the contextualist does incur a burden by advocating her semantic thesis.

One might think that the semantic burden facing the contextualist is easy to discharge. After all, it is well-nigh uncontroversial that certain epistemic terms conceptually related to 'know' are context-sensitive. Consider, for example, the use of 'might' as an epistemic modal. It is uncontroversial that a sentence such as 'President Clinton might have been in Florida sometime in 2004' is context-sensitive. Suppose Joe has no information bearing one way or another on Clinton's whereabouts in 2004. Then, what Joe would say by uttering this sentence is true. But, if Clinton utters this sentence, what he says would be false, since he knows perfectly well whether or not he was in Florida in 2004. So what this sentence expresses in Joe's mouth is different from what this sentence expresses in Clinton's mouth. The sentence expresses different propositions relative to different contexts of use, and is therefore clearly context-sensitive. One might therefore think that the claim that knowledge ascriptions are context-sensitive is equally uncontroversial.

However, the uncontroversial context-sensitivity of epistemic uses of 'might' is due to the fact that 'might' is relative to someone's evidential basis. Once we know *whose* evidence or

knowledge is relevant, we have resolved all of the context-sensitivity attending to an occurrence of 'might'. In short, the context-
sensitivity of 'might' is like the context-sensitivity of the term
'enemy'. In order to know what proposition is expressed by an
utterance of 'John is an enemy', I need to know of whom John is
said to be an enemy. Similarly, in order to know what proposition
is expressed by 'Bill Clinton might have been in Florida sometime
in 2004', I need to know whose evidence is in question. For a
claim that p is epistemically possible is a claim about some
person, to the effect that p is not obviously inconsistent with
what that person knows.[7] Once we know *which* person's knowledge is relevant for a claim of epistemic possibility, no more
contextual resolution is relevant for determining the proposition
expressed by that sentence.[8]

Knowledge ascriptions do not have a parallel kind of context-
sensitivity. For the question of whose knowledge is at issue in a
knowledge ascription does not arise. In contrast to claims of
epistemic possibility, this information is simply specified in the
subject of the knowledge ascription. That is, 'It might have rained
in New York on September 22, 2004' is context-sensitive because
we need to know whose knowledge is relevant in order to
determine the proposition expressed by an occurrence of the
sentence. But, in order to determine the proposition expressed
by 'Bill Clinton knows that it did not rain in New York on
September 22, 2004', we do not need to know whose knowledge
is in question. It is obviously *Bill Clinton*'s knowledge that
is relevant.

There is thus certainly no obvious route from the uncontroversial context-sensitivity of ascriptions of epistemic possibility to

[7] Cf. Hawthorne (2004: 26) and Stanley (2005a).

[8] Keith DeRose (1991) has argued that epistemic modals have additional
context-sensitivity. However, the argument for this position is no more intuitive
than the argument for the context-sensitivity of knowledge attributions, as
DeRose would admit. Therefore one cannot use this sort of context-sensitivity
in an effective argument for contextualism about knowledge attributions.

the context-sensitivity of knowledge ascriptions. One might think that there is an obvious route from the context-sensitivity of *other* constructions to the context-sensitivity of knowledge attributions. Contextualists typically tell us, when introducing the thesis, that it would not be at all surprising if predicates such as 'knows that Bush is president' turned out to be context-sensitive in the ways they describe. After all, we are told, many natural language predicates are context-sensitive. As Stewart Cohen (1999: 60) writes:

Many, if not most, predicates in natural language are such that the truth-value of sentences containing them depends on contextually determined standards, e.g. 'flat', 'bald', 'rich', 'happy', 'sad'.... These are all predicates that can be satisfied to varying degrees and that can also be satisfied simpliciter. So, e.g., we can talk about one surface being flatter than another and we can talk about a surface being flat simpliciter. For predicates of this kind, context will determine the degree to which the predicate must be satisfied in order for the predicate to apply simpliciter. So the context will determine how flat a surface must be in order to be flat.

Cohen's passage suggests that the burden of proof on someone who makes the semantic claim that a construction is context-sensitive is not high.

Context-sensitive expressions come in many distinct classes. They include (*a*) 'core' indexicals such as 'I', 'here', and 'now', (*b*) demonstratives such as 'this' and 'that', (*c*) gradable adjectives such as 'tall', 'flat', and 'large', (*d*) determiners such as 'many', (*e*) modal auxiliaries such as 'can', (*f*) relational expressions such as 'local' and 'enemy', (*g*) noun phrases such as 'every student' and 'most professors', and (*h*) adverbial quantifiers such as 'usually' and 'always'. Given the large array of context-sensitive constructions, Cohen's optimistic position that there is not a *high* degree of proof on the contextualist's shoulders is justified.

Cohen's optimism is further supported by the examples we have discussed in the Introduction. These examples involve ordinary intuitions about knowledge ascriptions. If we are to preserve (*a*) the semantic significance of our intuitions, and (*b*) the plausible theoretical thesis of intellectualism, the examples lead us to contextualism. So there is great plausibility to the context-ualist's methodology.

Nevertheless, I do not believe the contextualist analysis of knowledge ascriptions is ultimately correct. The argument for contextualism is not a pure argument from intuitions about cases. Rather, it is an argument from intuitions, together with the theoretical claim of intellectualism. Since I agree with the contextualist that we should preserve (*a*), the semantic signifi-cance of our intuitions, what I will ultimately reject is (*b*), the plausible theoretical thesis of intellectualism. That is, ultimately I will argue for an anti-intellectual account of knowledge, one that captures the intuitions we have about the cases we have dis-cussed, but does so by rejecting intellectualism.

My favored account involves rejecting a plausible theoretical thesis about knowledge. So I will have to show that the benefits of contextualism are illusory, and its costs substantial. I will argue that there is good evidence against the thesis that knowledge ascriptions are context-sensitive. I will also argue that context-ualism lacks many of the theoretical benefits it is supposed to possess. So, in the face of an alternative account of these intu-itions, one that violates only the thesis of intellectualism, con-textualism is undermined.

I will argue that, *except for the intuitions we have about the cases we have discussed*, there is no further evidence that knowledge ascriptions are context-sensitive in a distinctively epistemological way. I will argue for this thesis by noting a series of disanalogies between knowledge ascriptions and uncontroversial context-sensitive constructions. I will begin by discussing comparative adjectives. I devote a large amount of space to this putative analogy, because this is an analogy contextualists have stressed at great length.

It is no surprise that contextualists have emphasized an ana-logy between 'know' and adjectives such as 'tall' and 'flat'. On one natural way of presenting contextualism, it is the doctrine that the relations denoted by 'know', with respect to different contexts of use, come in higher and lower 'strengths'. In particular, for this sort of contextualist, the word 'know' has a content that is a function of the epistemic standards in the context. When Hannah finds out that she must deposit her check before the day is out, intuitively her evidence must satisfy a higher epistemic standard in order for her to know that the bank is open. The standard contextualist accounts for this by supposing that the word 'know' changes its content in the new context. It expresses a relation that Hannah stands in to a proposition only if her evidence for that proposition satisfies this higher epistemic standard.

For the contextualist, then, knowledge states come in higher or lower 'strengths'. Knowledge attributions are thus comparable to gradable expressions, such as adjectives like 'tall' and 'flat'. An attribution of tallness is sensitive to a contextually salient scale of height, as is an attribution of flatness. If what is at issue are basketball players, then that brings in one rather high standard for 'tall'; if what is at issue are fifth-graders, then that brings in a considerably lower standard for 'tall'. In this sense, one could speak of tallness relations coming in higher or lower 'strengths' as well. Many verbs are also gradable. For example, the verb 'like' is linked to a scale that allows us to speak of liking one person more than we like another person, or liking someone very much. So, if this standard contextualist semantics were correct, one would expect 'know' to behave like such an expression.

2

Knowledge Ascriptions and Gradability

The predicates mentioned by Cohen—the 'kind' of which he speaks in his second to last sentence—are not a disjunctive sort. They are *gradable adjectives*. These words are almost certainly context-sensitive. In talking about buildings, 'is tall' may express a property that it does not express when talking about people. Furthermore, gradable adjectives are context-sensitive in just the way that Cohen and DeRose claim that knowledge ascriptions are. According to Cohen and DeRose, knowledge ascriptions come in varying degrees of strength. In other words, knowledge ascriptions are intuitively *gradable*. Contextualists speak, as their theory suggests, of higher and lower standards for knowledge. Comparative adjectives are one natural kind of gradable expression. It is therefore no surprise that epistemologists since Unger (1975: ch. 2) and Lewis (1983) have been exploiting the analogy between 'know' and adjectives such as 'flat' and 'tall'. But, as I will argue in this section, the attempt to treat 'know' as a gradable expression fails. This casts suspicion upon the contextualist semantics for knowledge ascriptions. First, it shows that one cannot appeal to the context-sensitivity of adjectives to justify the context-dependence of knowledge ascriptions. Secondly, it casts doubt upon the claim that knowledge comes in varying degrees of strength, a core claim of many versions of contextualism.

There are two linguistic tests for gradability. First, if an expression is gradable, it should allow for modifiers. For example, predicative uses of comparative adjectives allow for modification, as in:

(1)(a) That is very flat.
   (b) That is really flat.
   (c) John is very tall.
   (d) John is really tall.

Secondly, if an expression is gradable, it should be conceptually related to a natural comparative construction. So, for 'flat', 'tall', and 'small' we have 'flatter than', 'taller than', and 'smaller than'. Both of these features are to be expected, if underlying the use of the relevant expression is a semantics involving degrees or intervals on a scale. For instance, the semantic effect of a modifier such as 'very' is to combine with a word such as 'tall' to yield a predicate whose threshold of application on the scale of height is higher than the threshold for 'tall'.[1]

The claim that knowledge ascriptions are gradable fits elegantly into the contextualist explanation for a version of High Stakes in which Hannah utters 'I guess I don't *really* know that the bank is open'. It is natural to read such uses of 'really' as degree modifiers, as in the examples in (1). That is, it is natural to read this kind of discourse as providing evidence for the gradability of 'know'. Over the course of the discourse, Hannah asserts that she knows that the bank is open, but also asserts

---

[1] Another feature of gradable expressions is that they can often occur with measure phrases. For instance, 'tall', 'wide', and 'old' co-occur with measure phrases, as in '5 feet tall', '2 feet wide', and '30 years old'. There is no natural measure phrase with 'know', even though it does not seem to be like the 'negative' comparative adjective, like 'flat', 'small', and 'young'. I will not pursue this disanalogy in what follows.

that she doesn't *really* know that the bank is open. That is like someone asserting that Bill is tall, but not *really* tall.

But the explanation of such occurrences of 'really' in terms of the gradability of knowledge is not correct. For negations of degree-modifier uses of 'really' can be conjoined with assertions of the unmodified forms without inconsistency:

(2)(*a*) John is tall, but not really tall.
   (*b*) Michigan is flat, but not really flat.

In contrast, the same facts do not hold of the use of 'really' when appended to a knowledge ascription:[2]

(3) #If the bank is open, then John knows that the bank is open, but doesn't really know that the bank is open.

The sentences in (2) are perfectly natural. In contrast, (3) is very odd. This suggests that the 'really' that occurs in the above description of the High Stakes is not a degree modifier.[3]

In fact, as I will now argue in detail, propositional knowledge ascriptions are not gradable at all. This conclusion has been noted

---

[2] A note on conventions: I will use three symbols to indicate varying kinds of infelicity. First, I use '#' for infelicity stemming from some non-grammatical source (say semantic or pragmatic oddity). Secondly, I use '*' to indicate ungrammaticality. Thirdly, I use '?' or '??' to indicate less than smooth grammatical acceptability. So, when a sentence is prefaced with '?', that indicates either that my informants found it somewhat, but not totally, grammatically unacceptable, or differed among one another as to its degree of acceptability.

[3] It appears that the use of 'really' when it occurs with knowledge ascriptions ('I don't really know that ...') is a *hedge*, in Paul Kay's sense. A hedge is some expression the linguistic function of which is to comment on the appropriateness of asserting the embedded sentence (as in uses of metalinguistic negation such as 'John isn't happy, he's ecstatic'). One such hedge, according to Kay, is the expression 'literally speaking', as in 'Literally speaking, that is pure water'. The occurrence of 'really' in knowledge ascriptions appears to be a hedge in this sense—in so using 'really', one concedes the infelicity of asserting that one knows the proposition in question. Note that this is consistent with it being perfectly true throughout that one knows that proposition.

before (Dretske 1981: ch. 5). However, the data surrounding knowledge ascriptions are rather complex. There are several constructions that suggest that knowledge ascriptions are, despite initial appearances, gradable. In the remainder of this chapter, I provide a complete case that knowledge ascriptions are not gradable, and draw some morals for contextualism about 'know'.

One might think that knowledge ascriptions are gradable on the basis of the obvious felicity of the following sort of construction:

(4)(a) John knows Bill better than Mary does.
　(b) Hannah knows logic better than John does.

But, in the sentences in (4), 'know' does not express a relation between a person and a proposition. These sentences are not propositional knowledge ascriptions; rather the occurrences of 'know' in them express the acquaintance relation, what would be expressed in German by *kennen* rather than *wissen*. It is only the gradability of propositional knowledge ascriptions that is at issue in contextualism in epistemology.

However, 'know' can marginally occur with 'very much' or less marginally with 'very well', as in:

(5)(a) ?John very much knows that Bush is president.
　(b) John knows very well that Bush is president.

But it is doubtful that these occurrences of 'very much' and 'very well' are genuine semantic modifiers of the knowing relation, rather than pragmatic indicators. In this sense, these constructions are similar to:

(6) 2 is very much an even number.

Evidence for this comes from several sources. First, note the unacceptability of negating the constructions in (7):

(7)(a) *John doesn't know very much that Bush is president.
　(b) *John doesn't know very well that Bush is president.

The unacceptability of the sentences in (7) contrasts with the naturalness of negating the verb phrase in a case in which 'very much' is clearly modifying the verb:

(8) I don't like Bill very much.

Secondly, 'know' is only with great awkwardness combined with 'very well' in non-assertoric speech acts. Contrast the sentences in (9) with (10):

(9)(a) ??Do you know very well that Bush is president?
   (b) *Do you know very much that Bush is president?
(10)   Do you like Bush very much?

So, the sentences in (5) are clearly not cases where the degree of knowing is operated on by 'very much' or 'very well'.

So 'very much' is not a way to modify the knowledge relation. The next question is whether there are comparative constructions involving 'know'. Certainly, such constructions are not formed with the use of the ordinary comparative 'more than':

(11)(a) ??John knows that Bush is president more than Sally knows it.
    (b) ??Hannah knows that Bush is president more than she knows that Clinton was president.

A far better case for a comparative construction involving 'know' exploits 'better than', as in:

(12) Hannah knows better than anyone that she is poor.

But the felicity of (12) does not entail that 'better than' is the comparative forming expression for 'know'.[4] For the expression

---

[4] Fred Dretske (2000: n. 1) writes, concerning such examples: 'I take such constructions to be describing not better knowledge, but more direct, more compelling kinds of evidence.' If Williamson (2000) is correct that evidence is knowledge, this is not a very good response.

'better than anyone' is *idiomatic*. For example, consider the oddity of:

(13)(*a*) ??Hannah knows better than three people that she is poor.

(*b*) ??Hannah knows better than Frank that she is poor.

So, 'better than anyone' is an idiomatic construction, one from which we can infer little about the semantics of 'know'.[5]

Furthermore, none of the non-philosopher informants I asked found the following acceptable, though they disagreed among themselves which was worst:

(14)(*a*) ??John knows that Bush is president better than Mary does.

(*b*) ??John knows that Bush is president better than Bill knows that Clinton is a Democrat.

In addition, all of my informants reported a strong difference in acceptability between these sentences, on the one hand, and the perfectly acceptable:

(15)(*a*) John likes Bill more than Mary does.

(*b*) John likes Bill more than Mary likes John.

So 'better than' is not a natural way to express comparisons between levels of epistemic position with 'know'. If the semantics of 'know' did involve scales of epistemic strength, then there should be uncontroversial examples of non-idiomatic comparisons and modifications.

One might think that these facts about 'know' have syntactic rather than semantic explanations. Perhaps sentences involving

---

[5] Indeed, 'better than anyone' seems like a positive polarity item idiom (like 'have a clue' is a negative polarity item idiom). It seems odd to say 'Hannah doesn't know better than anyone that she is poor'). As Nunberg, Sag, and Wasow (1994) emphasize, idiomaticity is a matter of degree, ranging from completely frozen idioms such as 'kick the bucket' to somewhat less frozen idioms. 'Knows better than anyone' is intermediate on the scale of idiomaticity.

intensifiers and comparisons with 'know' are deviant because 'know' is a verb that takes a sentential complement, and verbs that take sentential complements grammatically do not allow for comparisons or intensifiers. However, this reply is incorrect. There are verbs in the same syntactic and semantic category as 'know' that are clearly gradable. For example, the verb 'regret' is a factive verb in the same syntactic category as 'know'. As the following examples show, 'regret' is clearly gradable:

(16)(a) Hannah very much regrets that she is unemployed.
   (b) Hannah doesn't regret very much that she is un-
        employed.
   (c) Hannah regrets very much that she is unemployed.
   (d) Hannah regrets that she is unemployed very much.

Here, the degree of regret is clearly modified by 'very much'. Furthermore, 'regret' easily allows for comparisons:

(17) Hannah regrets that she is unemployed more than she
      regrets that she is unpopular.

This shows that the lack of straightforward comparatives or degree modifiers has nothing to do with the syntax, or even the factivity, of 'know'. There are syntactically and semantically similar expressions whose link to degrees and scales is uncontroversial.

The evidence concerning gradability is more complicated when one considers the deverbal adjective 'known'. But, even here, there does not appear to be a good case for a semantics involving a scale of *epistemic strength*. This adjective, unlike its verbal relative, does give rise to comparisons and modifications. But they are not of the relevant sort. So, for example, consider:

(18)(a) That broccoli is low fat is better known than that
        broccoli prevents cancer.
   (b) That broccoli is low fat is well known.

(18a) does not mean that there is more evidence that broccoli is low fat than that broccoli prevents cancer; rather, it means that the fact that broccoli is low fat is more *widely known* than the fact that broccoli prevents cancer. Similarly, (18b) means, not that there is a lot of evidence that broccoli is low fat, but that it is *widely known* that broccoli is low fat. Evidence for this hypothesis comes from the fact that, while (19a) is perfectly acceptable, (19b) sounds quite odd:

(19)(a) That broccoli prevents the flu is well known, but ill understood.
   (b) ?That broccoli prevents the flu is well known, though few people know it.

Furthermore, as Tamar Gendler (p.c.) has pointed out to me, instances of (20) are quite odd:

(20) It is well known that p, and less well known that q, but more people know that q than know that p.

These data are explicable on the assumption that the only available reading for 'well known' is widely known. So, while the data are more complex here, the adjectival relative of 'know', on the rare use of it where it expresses propositional knowledge, does not seem to be an obvious candidate for analysis via degrees on a scale of epistemic strength.

Another potential source of evidence for the gradability of 'know' comes from its use in certain kinds of embedded questions. Consider, for example:

(21)(a) John knows how to swim well.
   (b) John knows how to ride a bicycle better than Mary does.[6]
   (c) Hannah knows where Texas is better than John does.

It is quite plausible that these are attributions of propositional knowledge.[7] If so, one might think that this suggests that know-

---

[6] I owe example (21a) to Jeff King and (21b) to Jamie Tappenden.
[7] See Stanley and Williamson (2001).

ledge is gradable after all. However, in these cases, what are being compared are *answers to questions*. In each case, one person is said to have a better answer to a certain question than another; the answer Hannah has to the question 'Where is Texas?' is better, or more complete, than the answer John has.[8] So, embedded questions do not provide evidence for the gradability of knowledge claims.

One reaction I have heard to the above arguments I have given for the conclusion that knowledge is not gradable is to maintain that I have focused on the wrong model (see Halliday forthcoming). Instead of 'know' being analogous to 'flat' or 'tall', the contextualist claim is rather that 'know' is analogous to 'flat *enough*' or 'tall *enough*'. Unlike 'flat' and 'tall', 'flat enough' and 'tall enough' are not gradable, as the oddity of the following demonstrates:

(22)(a) ??That table is flatter enough than this table.
　　(b) ??That building is very tall enough.

If the contextualist claim is that the model for 'know' is 'tall enough' or 'flat enough', rather than 'tall' or 'flat', then the fact that knowledge is not gradable is no objection to it.

It is not clear to me in what sense 'know' is supposed to be analogous to 'tall enough', 'flat enough' or even 'justified enough'. There are all sorts of disanalogies between what the contextualist wants to say about 'know' and the behavior of 'tall enough', 'flat enough', and 'justified enough'. Most alarmingly, one standard use of these expressions is to convey that something has the property for a sufficient degree for present purposes, though it does not in fact have the property. For example, saying

---

[8] In the case of (21*a*), the 'well' modifies the swimming, rather than the knowledge. The claim can be represented as 'John knows [how to swim well]'. We can have felicitous uses of sentences such as 'John knows very well how to swim', where 'well' is made to apply to the knowledge relation. However, 'well', in such uses, is not a degree modifier; an utterance of such a sentence is felicitous only when used to deny the appearance or the claim that John does not know how to swim.

that something is *tall enough* usually gives rise to the implicature that the thing in question is not tall—that is, does not meet the contextually salient standards for 'tall'. Similarly, saying that something is flat enough often gives rise to the implicature that it does not meet the contextually salient standards for 'flat'. One can easily imagine a basketball coach defending a player's inclusion on a team, with:

(23) He isn't tall, but he is tall enough.

What the coach is saying is that the player in question may not be tall by basketball standards, but is tall enough to play his position competently. One sees similar behavior with 'justified enough', as in:

(24) I may not be justified in my suspicion, but I'm justified enough to investigate further.

If 'know' is supposed to be synonymous with something like 'is justified enough in one's true belief', then, just as one is able smoothly to say 'He's not justified, but he's justified enough', one would expect to be able smoothly to say things like:

(25) John isn't justified in his belief that the bank is open, but he knows that the bank is open.

But utterances of sentences such as (25) are extremely awkward, certainly more so than utterances of sentences such as (23) and (24). Furthermore, it would be absurd to argue that it is a *standard use* of an utterance of an instance of 'x knows that p' to convey that x is not justified that p. But one does standardly use instances of 'x is justified enough that p' to communicate that x is not justified that p. Therefore, 'know that p' simply does not behave as 'is justified enough in one's true belief that p'. These disanalogies are sufficient to undermine the plausibility of the proposal.[9]

---

[9] The contextualist might retreat here to 'at least justified enough'. But this too allows for straightforwardly felicitous utterances of (25), since one can be at least justified enough for certain purposes, without being justified.

The contextualist semantic claim is that 'know' is context-sensitive. Contextualists often write as if the prima facie case for the contextual sensitivity of 'know' is strong, citing the uncontroversial context-sensitivity of adjectives such as 'tall', 'flat', and 'small'. Their purpose in so doing is to shift the burden of proof from their shoulders to their opponents'; if 'many if not most predicates of natural language are context-dependent', then someone who claims that 'know' is context-dependent does not suffer from a large burden of proof. My point in this section has been to emphasize that these arguments do not suffice in the least to lift the burden of proof from the shoulders of the contextualist about 'know'. The fact that the semantic contents of comparative adjectives are sensitive to contextually salient standards is irrelevant to the claim that 'know' has a similar context-sensitive semantics.

If the envisaged analogy to expressions such as 'tall enough' had been plausible, it would threaten a stronger conclusion that can now be drawn from the above discussion. Natural language expressions that are semantically linked to degrees on scales exploit this link in a variety of recognizable ways—by allowing for comparisons between degrees on the scale, and by allowing modifications of the contextually salient degree on the scale. If, as on some versions of contextualism, the semantic content of 'know' were sensitive to contextually salient standards, and hence linked to a scale of epistemic strength (as 'tall' is linked to a scale of height), then we should expect this link to be exploited in a host of different constructions, such as natural comparatives. The fact that we do not see such behavior should make us at the very least suspicious of the claim of such a semantic link. Thus, an investigation into the context-sensitivity of predicates such as 'is tall', 'is small', and their ilk adds to, rather than removes, the burden of proof on contextualists about 'know'.

However, our discussion in this chapter threatens only certain versions of contextualism, namely those that appeal to a 'comparative-adjective' model of different knowledge relations. According to the comparative-adjective model, knowledge relations are ordered according to epistemic strength, as tallness or intelligence is ordered according to (not necessarily linear) scales. But a contextualist may choose a different model (for a useful discussion of this point, see Gillies forthcoming). On some of these models, there may not even be a partial ordering among the different knowledge relations that are denoted by the term 'know', relative to an occasion of use. For example, someone may propose that one occurrence of 'know' requires an agent to have special evidence against one set of possibilities in order to stand in the denoted relation to a proposition, whereas another occurrence of 'know' might require an agent to have special evidence against another set of possibilities. Perhaps the possibilities in one set are not more remote than the possibilities in another set; they are just different possibilities. On this model, the context-sensitivity of 'know' would be more like the context-sensitivity of quantified expressions. We therefore would not necessarily expect knowledge ascriptions to be gradable. So, in the next chapter, I turn to a broader discussion of the evidence available for the contextualist claim, one that generalizes to other potential models for the alleged context-sensitivity of instances of 'know that p'.

3

Knowledge Ascriptions and Context-Sensitivity

I have argued that knowledge ascriptions are not intuitively gradable. There are two morals to the discussion. First, if one is a contextualist, one should avoid adopting a version of contextualism that makes knowledge semantically scalar. Secondly, the contextualist thesis about knowledge ascriptions is not supportable by appeal to an analogy to gradable expressions. In this section, I will argue that the alleged context-sensitivity of knowledge ascriptions has no other parallel among the class of uncontroversial context-sensitive expressions. During the course of these arguments, we will also see that some of the alleged theoretical benefits of contextualism are illusory. The way I will support this final thesis is by arguing that, if knowledge ascriptions are context-sensitive, then we would expect them to behave in ways that run counter to the contextualist's claims.

Contextualists have generally chosen to implement their claims semantically via the view that the verb 'know' is an indexical:

Thus the theory I wish to defend construes 'knowledge' as an indexical. As such, one speaker may attribute knowledge to a subject while another speaker denies knowledge to that subject, without contradiction. (Cohen 1988: 97)

Citing this passage, DeRose (1992: 920–1) writes:

This lack of contradiction is the key to the sense in which the knowledge attributor and the knowledge denier mean something different by 'know'. It is similar to the sense in which two people who think they are in the same room but are in fact in different rooms talking to each other over an intercom mean something different by 'this room' when one claims, 'Frank is not in this room' and the other insists, 'Frank is in this room—I can see him!' There is an important sense in which both do mean the same thing by 'this room', in which they are using the phrase in the same sense. But there is also an important sense in which they do not mean the same thing by the phrase; this is the sense by which we can explain the lack of contradiction between what the two people are saying. To use David Kaplan's terminology, the phrase is being used with the same character, but with different content. Similarly, in [a bank case] . . . when, in the face of my wife's doubt, I admit that I don't know that the bank will be open on Saturday, I don't contradict an earlier claim to know that I might have made before the doubt was raised and before the issue was so important because, in an important sense, I don't mean the same thing by 'know' as I meant in the earlier claim: While 'know' is being used with the same *character*, it is *not* being used with the same *content*. Or so the contextualist will claim.

Similarly, Lewis (1996: 564) writes:

in the skeptical argument the context switched midway, and the semantic-value of the context-dependent word 'know' switched with it.

So, Cohen, DeRose, and Lewis have all implemented their contextualist claims via the view that the verb 'know' is an indexical in Kaplan's sense, having different semantic values relative to different contexts.[1] In recent years, however, some

---

[1] DeRose provides a reason for contextualists to advocate an indexical treatment of 'know'. According to him, so doing allows the contextualist to respond to the charge that she is committed to the truth of utterances of

contextualists have moved beyond the model of contextualism that treats the word 'know' itself as an indexical expression, like 'here' or 'now' (e.g. Schaffer 2004; Ludlow 2005). My purpose in this section is to provide some empirical arguments to show that, if instances of 'know that p' are context-sensitive in a distinctively epistemological way, their context-sensitivity is not 'detectable' by means that would detect the context-sensitivity of a range of other expressions. Some of the arguments I provide below suggest that the indexical model of 'know' is not correct. But I will not confine myself to considering only the indexical model of 'know'. Instead, I seek to show disanalogies between knowledge ascriptions and a wide variety of context-sensitive constructions.

At the outset, I should confess to some skepticism about the existence of a single property that all context-sensitive expressions have, and all non-context-sensitive expressions lack (other than the property of context-sensitivity). The attempts that I am aware of for establishing such tests fail rather dramatically at their intended task. It is instructive to look at one test recently proposed by Herman Cappelen and Ernie Lepore, which they call *The Collective Description Test*. According to Cappelen and Lepore (2005: 99):

If for a range of true utterances of the form 'A v-s' and 'B v-s' we obviously can describe what they have in common by using 'v' (i.e. by using 'A and B v'), then that's evidence in favor of the view that 'v' in these different utterances has the same semantic content, and hence, is not context-sensitive.

Cappelen and Lepore use the Collective Description Test to argue that a range of apparently context-sensitive constructions are not after all context-sensitive. For example, they use it to argue that 'is tall' is not context-sensitive. Suppose that John utters 'Jill is tall' and Bill utters 'Mary is tall'. One can conclude from the two premises they provide that 'Both Jill and Mary are

sentences such as 'I don't know that I have hands, but I used to know that I have hands.' (cf. DeRose 1992: 924–8; 2000). I challenge DeRose's arguments below.

tall'. By the collective description test, then, 'is tall' is not context-sensitive. Similarly, suppose John utters 'Jill knows that penguins waddle', and Bill utters 'Mary knows that penguins waddle'. One can conclude from the two premises they provide that Jill and Mary know that penguins waddle, and hence, if the Collective Description Test is reliable, that 'knows that penguins waddle' is not context-sensitive.

Consider two sisters, Jill and Mary. John utters 'Jill loves her mother' and Bill utters 'Mary loves her mother'. One can conclude from the two premises offered that 'Each sister loves her mother.' Since one can describe what Jill and Mary have in common by the verb phrase 'loves her mother', it follows that Cappelen and Lepore's test falsely predicts that 'loves her mother' is not context-sensitive. Similarly, suppose Jill utters 'I love my mother' and Mary utters 'I love my mother'. Jill and Mary can now conclude in unison, 'We love our mothers'. Cappelen and Lepore's test appears falsely to predict that 'loves my mother' is not context-sensitive.[2]

Cappelen and Lepore might understandably respond by arguing that 'loves her mother' in John and Bill's utterance is not context-sensitive, but is rather a case of controlled anaphora, where 'her' is *bound* (by some higher operator, e.g. a lambda operator associated with the verb phrase). They could also give the same response for 'love my mother', in Jill and Mary's utterances of 'I love my mother'. But this claim, though well motivated, is not open to Cappelen and Lepore. For then their opponents can give the *very same response* to defuse Cappelen and

---

[2] One cannot complain that 'love their mother' is not the same verb phrase as 'loves my mother' (because 'their' is plural case and 'my' is singular case). For in some of Cappelen and Lepore's target examples, we find the exact same situation. For example, 'know that penguins waddle' is plural, in 'Jill and Mary know that penguins waddle', whereas 'knows that penguins waddle' is singular, in 'Jill knows that penguins waddle'. But Cappelen and Lepore still infer from the fact that one can collect with 'know that penguins waddle', to the conclusion that 'knows that penguins waddle' is not context-sensitive

Lepore's application of the Collective Description Test to their favored examples.

For example, one of their targets is the view, espoused in Ludlow (1989) and Stanley (2000, 2002), that predicative uses of adjectives, such as 'is tall', are associated with comparison class variables. But, if Cappelen and Lepore are allowed to give the above response to defend their test, advocates of such a view could give the exact same response to explain why one can, from utterances of 'Jill is tall' and 'Mary is tall' draw the conclusion 'Both Jill and Mary are tall'.[3]

So, either Cappelen and Lepore's test fails as a test of context-sensitivity, or it cannot be employed against their intended targets. I think it is no accident that their test fails. I doubt that there is one test that perspicuously divides all context-sensitive terms into one category, and all non-context-sensitive terms into another category. There are too many different classes of context-sensitive expressions. But what I am in a position to provide is a good inductive case that knowledge ascriptions are not context-sensitive in a distinctively epistemological way, as the contextualist would have it. In the realm of the empirical, a good inductive case is all we can expect.

There are a few tests that detect the context-sensitivity of a range of context-sensitive expressions that do not detect the alleged context-sensitivity of instances of 'know that p'. These

---

[3] For example, in Stanley (2002), I argue that predicative uses of adjectives, such as 'is tall', have the syntactic structure 'is tall $f(i)$'. In these representations, 'f' denotes a function from objects to comparison classes, whose value is supplied by context, and 'i' denotes an individual, relative to a context. Both 'f' and 'i' can be bound by higher operators. So an utterance of the sentence 'Jill is tall' is really of the form 'Jill$_i$ is tall $f(i)$', and an utterance of the sentence 'Mary is tall' is really of the form 'Mary$_i$ is tall $g(i)$.' On the envisaged response from Cappelen and Lepore, variables inside a verb phrase can be bound by operators attaching to the Verb Phrase (this is what they would have to say to defend the view that 'her' and 'my' are instances of bound anaphora). So, the reason one could conclude 'Both Jill and Mary are tall' from an utterance of 'Jill is tall' and 'Mary is tall' is because it is of the form 'Both Jill and Mary λx (are tall $h(x)$)', where the value of 'h', relative to the envisaged context, is a function that takes Jill onto f(Jill), and takes Mary onto g(Mary).

tests involve speech-act reports and propositional anaphora. It would be a mistake to place excessive weight upon these tests. For the context-sensitivity of certain constructions that are clearly context-sensitive is also not detectable by these tests. I include these tests, not because 'passing' them is a necessary condition for context-sensitivity, but because they are one part of the larger inductive argument that instances of 'knows that p' are not context-sensitive. I will then try to motivate a more general property of context-sensitive expressions, and conclude by arguing that instances of 'know that p' lack this more general property.

Here is the first kind of argument. Suppose A and B are at the zoo. A is a non-philosopher, and B is a philosophy professor, trying to explain what epistemology is to A. B asks A to give her an example of a proposition that A takes herself to know, in response to which B will explain how to give a skeptical undermining of A's knowledge. Here is a discourse in this situation that should, if 'know' is like a core indexical such as 'I', 'here', and 'now', sound perfectly reasonable (certainly, according to the contextualist, every statement in the discourse is true):

zoo
A. (looking at a zebra in a normal zoo). I know that is a zebra.
B. But can you rule out its being a cleverly painted mule?
A. I guess I can't rule that out.
B. So you admit that you don't know that's a zebra, and so you were wrong earlier?
A. I didn't say I did. I wasn't considering the possibility that it could be a cleverly painted mule.

A's final utterance, according to the contextualist's semantics, is perfectly true. But this seems a very strange result. It is extremely difficult to make sense of A's denial except as a lie. But instead the contextualist predicts that it is clearly true.

The behavior of 'know' in this kind of discourse contrasts with some other clearly context-sensitive expressions. For example, modal expressions are context-sensitive. In the first instance, there are what some philosophers have thought of as different 'senses' of possibility, such as physical possibility, logical possibility, epistemic possibility, and metaphysical possibility.[4] But, even fixing upon one sense of modality, there are different readings of a modal term such as 'could', depending upon the context of use. For example, where 'could' is interpreted as physical possibility, one might mean physical possibility in a more or less restricted sense. Suppose A is in a conversation with a group of people talking about innovations in flight that have not been marketed to the public. B overhears A's comment, without knowing the background conversation:

TECHNOLOGY

A. It's possible to fly from London to New York City in 30 minutes.

B. That's absurd! No flights available to the public today would allow you to do that. It's not possible to fly from London to New York City in 30 minutes.

A. I didn't say it was. I wasn't talking about what's possible given what is available to the public, but rather what is possible given all existing technology.

In contrast to the last line of ZOO, A's final comment in TECHNOLOGY seems perfectly appropriate, and indeed true. The worry for the contextualist is that the discourse in ZOO should be as plausible and coherent as the discourse in TECHNOLOGY. But it clearly is not. This is a good minimal pair that shows that the alleged context-sensitivity of instances of 'know that p' is considerably less accessible to us than the context-sensitivity of modals. This should lead us to doubt models according to which the context-sensitivity of 'know' is modeled upon the context-sensitivity of modal expressions.

---

[4] The degree to which this marks genuine ambiguity or a kind of indexicality is subject to dispute; see Kratzer (1977).

One should be clear about the strategy here. I am not arguing, as others have, that the infelicity of a discourse such as zoo by itself undermines contextualism. By providing the contrasting minimal pair zoo and TECHNOLOGY, my purpose is just to reveal differences between some uncontroversial context-sensitive expressions, such as modals, with instances of 'know that p'. The contrast between zoo and TECHNOLOGY is not an anti-contextualist silver bullet, but rather one piece of the overall inductive argument for the thesis that the only evidence for the context-sensitivity of instances of 'know that p' is the cases discussed in the Introduction.

Contextualism also makes some strange predictions about propositional anaphora. Consider the following discourses:

(1) If I have hands, then I know that I have hands. But come to think of it, I might be a brain in a vat, in which case I would believe I have hands, but wouldn't. Now that I'm considering such a skeptical possibility seriously, even if I have hands, I don't know that I do. But what I said earlier is still true.[5]

According to the contextualist semantics, there should be a clearly true reading of all the sentences in these two discourses. But they are very difficult to grasp. In particular, the only interpretation for

[5] The reason I have placed the initial sentence in conditional form is that, if the initial sentence was just 'I know that I have hands', the contextualist could explain the infelicity of the final utterance by appeal to the knowledge account of assertion. Let us use 'know-L' for the lower-standards knowledge relation and 'know-H' for the higher-standards knowledge relation. Suppose that the initial sentence were just 'I know that I have hands'. Asserting that one's previous claim to know-L that one has hands is still true clearly entails that one has hands. By the knowledge account of assertion (the norm for assertion is knowledge), I could assert in the higher standard's context that my previous knowledge claim is still true only if I know-H that I know-L that I have hands. But this requires that I know-H that I have hands (by an uncontroversial application of single-premise epistemic closure). But, by stipulation, I do not know-H that I have hands. So a contextualist could explain the infelicity of the final utterance by appeal to the knowledge account of assertion. By placing the original sentence in conditional form, I have blocked this maneuver.

the expression 'what I said' in the final sentence is the proposition whose truth is being denied in the previous sentence.[6]

The case is again markedly different with uncontroversial context-sensitive expressions, such as genuine indexicals:

(2) It is raining here. Had I been inside, what I said still would have been true. But now that I am in fact inside, it is not raining here.

When informed of the facts, there is a clear reading of all of the sentences in (2) where they are true.

So, certain tests that detect the context-sensitivity of modal expressions and obvious indexicals are blind to the alleged context-sensitivity of instances of 'knows that p'. Mark Richard (2004: 236) presses the worry, in response to the above arguments, that these tests are also blind to the context-sensitivity of obvious context-sensitive constructions, such as those involving comparative adjectives. Commenting on my contrast between ZOO and TECHNOLOGY, Richard writes:

The following dialogue is exactly as bizarre . . .
A. He is rich.
B. He can't afford a house on the Vineyard.
A. I see your point.
B. So you admit you were wrong when you said he was rich.
A. I said no such thing.

I agree with Richard that the above considerations may very well not be infallible indicators of context-sensitivity. But I disagree with Richard's particular example. I do think that the tests

---

[6] DeRose appears to concede the point that, on his view, a metalinguistic version of this discourse is fine. Speaking of just such a case, DeRose (1992: 925) writes: '[one] can say, "My previous knowledge claim was true," just as one can say, "My previous location claim was true." Or so I believe. But saying these things would have a point only if one were interested in the truth-value of the earlier claim, rather than in the question of whether in the present contextually determined sense one knew and knows, or didn't and doesn't.' But it does not seem that semantic ascent helps here.

are successful in detecting the context-sensitivity of constructions involving gradable adjectives. For Richard's exchange with 'rich' is simply not parallel to ZOO and TECHNOLOGY. In the cases of ZOO and TECHNOLOGY, background context is provided to make A's final assertion more palatable. For example, in the case of ZOO, A adds to 'I didn't say I did', the helpful explanation 'I wasn't considering the possibility that it could be a cleverly painted mule'. In the case of TECHNOLOGY, A adds to 'I didn't say it was', the helpful explanation 'I wasn't talking about what's possible given what is available to the public, but rather what is possible given all existing technology'. The additional background context rescues the felicity of A's assertion in TECHNOLOGY, but does nothing to rescue the felicity of A's assertion in ZOO. Adding similar background context to Richard's 'rich' dialogue rescues the felicity of A's final assertion:

RICH
A. He is rich.
B. He can't afford a house on the Vineyard.
A. I see your point.
B. So you admit you were wrong when you said he was rich.
A. I didn't say that. I wasn't considering that level of wealth.

Perhaps the background context in RICH does not make A's assertion 'I didn't say that' as smooth as A's assertion 'I didn't say it was' in TECHNOLOGY. But RICH is still far more similar to TECHNOLOGY than it is to ZOO. In ZOO, A's final assertion is well-nigh incoherent to the ordinary speaker, whereas RICH is perfectly coherent to everyone.

So, I do not think that Richard has succeeded in undermining these tests as reliable indicators of context-sensitivity. Nevertheless, I am prepared to admit that the above tests are not perfectly reliable indicators, for the simple reason that I doubt that there are *any* perfectly reliable indicators of context-sensitivity. The next piece of my inductive argument against the contextualist is not such a test for context-sensitivity, but rather a generalization about the nature of semantic context-sensitivity. I am not certain whether this generalization is true. But it seems both empirically well confirmed, and motivated by general considerations about the nature of semantic context-sensitivity. And, if it is a true generalization, it provides further evidence against contextualism as a position in epistemology.

In the first instance, it is individual words that are context-sensitive, not sentences or discourses. For example, the semantic context-sensitivity of the sentence 'I am human' is traceable to the semantically context-sensitive word 'I'. Similarly, the semantic context-sensitivity of 'She is tired' is traceable to the word 'She', which is context-sensitive, and the present tense. In some constructions, the semantic context-sensitivity is traceable to an unpronounced element in the syntactic structure of a sentence. For example, the semantic context-sensitivity of 'John is tall' may be traceable to an unpronounced element in the syntactic structure of the predicate 'is tall', say a comparison class variable associated with the adjective 'tall' (see Stanley 2000). But in these instances, too, context-sensitivity is traceable to an individual element in the sentence uttered, albeit one that is not pronounced.

This suggests the following generalization. Since semantic context-sensitivity is traceable to an individual element, multiple occurrences of that element in a discourse should be able to take on differing values. In the case of an utterance such as 'This is larger than this', where two different objects are pointed to by the person uttering the sentence, this feature is obviously confirmed. But it is present in a broader range of constructions.

For example, suppose John, who is very small for his age, identifies with small things. He has a picture on the wall in his bedroom of an elephant fighting off a much larger elephant. He also has a framed tiny butterfly on his wall. When he is asked why he has both things hung up, he says:

(3) That butterfly is small, and that elephant is small.

John in fact also has a fondness for flat things. On his wall is a picture of a field in Kansas, and on his desk is a rock. When asked why he has both, he replies:

(4) That field is flat, and this rock is flat.

Now imagine a picture of a butterfly that is surrounded by much smaller butterflies; it is huge for a butterfly. It is next to a picture of an elephant that is surrounded by much larger elephants. The following is a good description of the situation:

(5) That butterfly is large, but that elephant isn't large.[7]

There are different possible explanations of why the two different occurrences of 'large' in (5) express different semantics values. For example, one might argue that the comparison class property for the first occurrence of 'large' is determined linguistically by the noun 'butterfly', and the second occurrence of 'large' is determined linguistically by the noun 'elephant' (see Ludlow 1989). Alternatively, one might think that 'large' is associated with different comparison class properties by free contextual assignment, in much the same way that unbound pronouns such as 'he' and 'she' have their denotations determined in context. The generalization is independent of either of these explanations. For the generalization is that, in the case of any context-sensitive expression, different occurrences of that expression can receive different values within a discourse by *whatever* mechanism, be it binding or contextual supplementation. And that is what we have seen to be the case for comparative adjectives.

It is worth expending a little more space on this example, since the proper interpretation of comparative adjectives is a vexed matter. In other work (Stanley 2002), I have argued for the

---

[7] It is worth mentioning that one can felicitously assign different standards to different occurrences of the same adjective, even when predicated of the same object; consider: 'In Michigan, that mountain is tall, but in Colorado, it would not be tall'.

following account of predicative uses of comparative adjectives. The syntactic structure of a predicate such as 'is tall' or 'is smart' contains a variable position, which can be either bound or free. When it is free, its value, relative to a context, is a comparison class property. Comparison class properties can be determined by the head noun, as in a reading of 'That butterfly is large', where it expresses the proposition that the butterfly in question is a large butterfly. Comparison class properties can also be determined by assorted extralinguistic factors.

Comparison class properties do not need to be kind properties. Though she would not construe them this way, Graff (2000) provides examples in which the comparison class for 'is old' can either be the property of *being a dog*, or be the property of *being an old dog* (suppose we are confronted with a 20-year-old dog; compared with several 14-year-old dogs, the 20-year-old dog is old, i.e. old for an old dog). Another example Graff (2000: 67) provides is as follows:

it can be appropriate for me to say, when I see my young nephew for the first time in months at a family gathering, 'Derek, you're so tall'. It can be appropriate for me to say this even though I know that my nephew has always been and still is short for his age. What I am saying is that he has significantly more height than I expected him to have, given what his height was the last time I saw him.

In this example, the comparison class property is the property of *being a height that Delia expected her nephew to be*. What Graff says, in uttering 'Derek, you're so tall', is that Derek is tall relative to the height that Graff expected her nephew to be.[8]

So, on the theory of gradable adjectives that I favor, they are associated with variables for comparison class properties. Examples such as (3)–(5) show that different occurrences of the

---

[8] I am using Graff's examples for a purpose she explicitly repudiates, since Graff herself (2000: 55) thinks that 'it is not the case that variation of the standards in use for a vague expression is always attributable to some comparison class'. However, Graff assumes that comparison classes must be kinds of some type, an assumption I reject.

same gradable adjective within a sentence can be associated with different comparison class properties. But the point that different occurrences of the same gradable adjective can be associated with different standards can be made on other accounts of gradable adjectives. For example, if one holds that gradable adjectives are associated with degrees on a scale, then examples such as (3)–(5) show that different occurrences of the same gradable adjective can be associated with different degrees on the relevant scale.[9]

This sort of shift is present in a variety of context-sensitive expressions other than gradable adjectives. For example, we see this behavior with demonstratives, context-sensitive determiners, and quantified noun phrases. For the first, as we have already seen, there is the example:

(6) That is larger than that.

For the second, consider:

(7) In Atlanta, there are many serial killers but not many unemployed men.

In this case, the contextual determinants for the denotation of 'many' change within a clause. The first occurrence of 'many' denotes a more distinct determiner meaning than the second occurrence of 'many', since (7) may be true even though there are many more unemployed men than serial killers. The same phenomenon occurs with quantified expressions, as (8) can express the proposition that every sailor on one ship waved to every sailor on another (Stanley and Williamson 1995: 294):

(8) Every sailor waved to every sailor.

[9] On my favored account of predicate uses of gradable adjectives (such as 'John is tall' or 'Mary is rich'), the degree on the scale is determined by the comparison class property. Many people have argued that the degree on the scale is not so determined (e.g. Richard 2004), but I am not convinced by these arguments.

It is no surprise that different occurrences of one and the same context-sensitive expression can have different values within the same discourse. For context-sensitivity is linked not to the *discourse*, but to a particular context-sensitive *term*. So what one is speaking about when one speaks of the 'standard of tallness' relevant for evaluating a particular use of 'is tall' is simply the degree of tallness that is associated with the expression 'tall' by whatever semantic mechanism one exploits.

Let us see how this point applies to the version of contextualism advocated in Lewis (1996). According to Lewis, the semantics of the word 'know' invokes universal quantification over possibilities. Lewis then exploits facts about natural language universal quantification to motivate contextualism about 'know':

> Finally, we must attend to the word 'every'. What does it mean to say that every possibility in which not-P is eliminated? An idiom of quantification, like 'every', is normally restricted to some limited domain. If I say that every glass is empty, so it's time for another round, doubtless I and my audience are ignoring most of all the glasses there are in the whole wide world throughout all of time. They are outside the domain. They are irrelevant to the truth of what was said.
>
> Likewise, if I say that every uneliminated possibility is one in which P, or words to that effect, I am doubtless ignoring some of all the uneliminated alternative possibilities that there are. They are outside the domain. They are irrelevant to the truth of what was said. (Lewis 1996: 553)

So, Lewis deduces contextualism about 'know' first, from the claim that 'know' involves universal quantification over possibilities, and secondly, from the fact that natural language quantification is typically restricted. But (as (8) demonstrated) it is a well-established fact that different occurrences of the same quantified expression within a discourse can be associated with different domains (Soames 1986: 357; Stanley and Williamson 1995: 294; Stanley and Szabo 2000: 249). Lewis's contextualism flows in part from facts about natural language quantification. So, two different occurrences of 'know' within the same discourse should be able to be associated with different sets of possibilities (say, a set including quite remote possibilities, and a set including only quite close possibilities).

Distinct occurrences of the same context-sensitive term can have different interpretations within a discourse. We should therefore expect distinct occurrences of the instances of 'know that p' to allow for the possibility of distinct interpretations within a discourse. But this opens the contextualist up to a number of objections that she does not otherwise face. Furthermore, if this is so, some of what contextualists say about the virtues of their theories over other theories falls by the wayside. I will substantiate these points in turn.

If instances of 'know that p' behave like comparative adjectives, quantifier phrases, context-sensitive determiners, or modals, then we would expect it to be smoothly acceptable to associate different standards of knowledge with different occurrences of the 'know that p', just as we associate different degrees of height with different occurrences of the predicate 'is tall'. So, if contextualism were true, we should expect the following to be fine:

(9) If there is an external world, many normal non-philosophers know that there is, but, by contrast, no epistemologists know that there is.

If 'know that there is an external world' could be associated with different standards, then one would expect an utterance of (9) to be felicitous and true, just as utterances of (3)–(8) are. For 'is large' means one thing when predicated of a butterfly, and quite another when predicated of an elephant. Similarly, 'many' means one thing when it occurs with 'unemployed men', and quite another when it occurs with 'serial killers'. So, if 'know that there is an external world' is context-sensitive in a similar manner, one would naturally expect it to have different contents when predicated of non-epistemologists and epistemologists.[10]

[10] Again, it is irrelevant whether the mechanism that would so affect the interpretation of the two distinct occurrences of 'know' is due to a parameter associated with 'know' being controlled by the noun phrases 'many normal

In responding to various objections, contextualists have exploited the view that distinct occurrences of 'know' within a discourse must be associated with the same standard. For example, this view is at work in the solution contextualists have provided to puzzles like the 'Now You Know it, Now You Don't' concern (Yourgrau 1983; DeRose 1992, 2000). This concern is that the contextualist semantics would allow for discourses such as:

KNOWLEDGE SHIFT

A. If that is a zebra, I know it is a zebra.
B. But can you rule out its being merely a cleverly painted mule?
A. No, I can't.
B. So you admit you didn't know it was a zebra?
A. If that is a zebra, then I knew it was a zebra. But now, after your question, even if it is a zebra, I don't know it is a zebra.[11]

DeRose (1992: 925) writes in response to a similar objection (similar because not in conditional form):

How shall the contextualist respond? The objection . . . is based upon a mistake. The contextualist believes that certain aspects of the context of an attribution or denial of knowledge attribution affect its content. . . . If in the context of the conversation the possibility of painted mules has been mentioned, and if the mere mention of this possibility has an effect on the conditions under which someone can be truly said to 'know', then any use of 'know' (or its past tense) is so affected, even a use in which one describes one's past condition.

This response presupposes that distinct occurrences of 'know' within a discourse must all be associated with the same standard.

non-philosophers' and 'no epistemologists', or due rather to a shift in free contextual assignment initiated by the use of these noun phrases.

[11] Again, I have placed this discourse in conditional form to avoid appeal to the knowledge account of assertion in explaining the infelicity of asserting in a higher-standards context that one's previous knowledge claim is true.

But the analogous claim is incorrect for uncontroversial context-sensitive expressions.

Consider, for example, a gradable adjective such as 'tall'. The parallel claim for 'tall' to DeRose's claim about 'know' would be that merely mentioning, for example, basketball players would so affect the conditions under which someone can be truly said to be 'tall', that any use of 'tall' is so affected, even a use in which one describes one's past condition. But this is clearly false for 'tall', as the following discourse suggests. Suppose that A was the tallest member of his seventh-grade class. But A didn't grow over the summer, and most of his classmates did. B is the eighth-grade teacher:

TALLNESS SHIFT
B. OK, A, you're average height, so you sit in the middle.
A. But last year, I was tall and I got used to sitting in the back.

In the case of a predicate such as 'is tall', one can clearly shift the standard governing it from a higher standard to a lower past standard. If the expression 'know that p' is context-sensitive, one should expect the very same behavior. That is, one should expect KNOWLEDGE SHIFT to be felicitous. DeRose's account of the infelicity of KNOWLEDGE SHIFT therefore presupposes that 'know' must be associated with the same standards throughout a discourse.

Shifting to Lewis's restricted quantification model of contextualism does not help to substantiate the contextualist's claim that raising a possibility to salience affects all future uses of 'know'. The parallel claim for quantification would be that once one introduces a domain of a certain size, a future use of a quantifier within that discourse cannot be understood to be restricted to a subset of that domain.[12] But this claim is quite clearly false:

---

[12] This is, in essence, the parallel pragmatic principle to Lewis's 'Rule of Attention' (1996: 559 ff.) for quantifier domain restriction.

A. Every van Gogh painting is in the Dutch National Museum.
B. That's a change. When I visited last year, I saw every Van Gogh painting, and some were definitely missing.

The domain for the first occurrence of the quantifier phrase 'every Van Gogh painting' is (if you like) maximally large. But we can, with no difficulty at all, understand the domain for the second occurrence to be a subset of this domain, restricted to last year's collection in the Dutch National Museum.[13] Lewis (1983: 247) claims that 'the boundary readily shifts outward if what is said requires it, but does not so readily shift inward if what is said requires that'. This claim, so important to his account of skepticism, is clearly false for domain restriction, the model upon which his account of 'know' is based.

DeRose (1992) also appeals to a direct analogy between the indexical 'here' and 'know' to defend his claim concerning the pragmatics of 'know':

Knowledge claims, then, can be compared to other sentences containing other context-sensitive words, like 'here'. One hour ago, I was in my office. Suppose I truly said, 'I am here'. Now I am in the word processing room. How can I truly say where I was an hour ago? I cannot truly say, 'I was here', because I wasn't here; I was there. The meaning of 'here' is fixed by the relevant contextual factors (in this case, my location) of the utterance, not by my location at the time being talked about.

The values of core indexicals, unlike most other context-sensitive expressions, are sometimes held to be fixed by facts about the context of utterance that are independent of speaker intentions (e.g. Wettstein (1984) on 'pure indexicals'). So, for example, the value of 'here' is fixed (in part) by the *place of utterance*, and the value of 'I' is fixed by *the person who utters it*. Perhaps then, by

---

[13] Of course, many Van Gogh paintings are housed in the Van Gogh museum in Amsterdam.

analogy, the standard of knowledge (unlike the standard of tallness) is fixed by a fact about the context of utterance that is independent of the intentions of the person making the knowledge ascription.

The analogy is of little help to the contextualist. First, as we have already demonstrated, the analogy between 'know' and core indexicals is poor. The context-sensitivity of core indexicals is easily demonstrable by a variety of tests, none of which detects the context-sensitivity of knowledge ascriptions. Secondly, the fact that the analogy is poor is problematic for the contextualist, since arguably core indexicals are the *only* expressions whose values are fixed (to some degree) independently of the intentions of the speaker. Third, it is not a *semantic* fact about core indexicals that they generally have the same denotation within a short discourse. It is rather a consequence of mundane physical facts about humans. Different occurrences of 'here' within a discourse tend to have the same denotation, because most of our conversations occur while remaining in the same location.[14] Different occurrences of 'I' within a single sentence tend to have the same denotation, because speakers rarely change mid-sentence. There is no reason to think that analogous mundane physical facts determine the same standard of knowledge throughout a discourse.

Once one abandons the contextualist claim that distinct occurrences of instances of 'know that *p*' in a single discourse must be associated with the same standards, the contextualist is open to the objection that, by contextualist lights, infelicitous discourses such as KNOWLEDGE SHIFT should be acceptable. On my view, this is not a terrible concession. For the contextualist has no response to the infelicity of very similar discourses, such

[14] There is a commercial for McDonald's that shows a woman driving with her children, which begins with the children requesting, 'Can we go to McDonald's now?', which is answered in the negative. Every subsequent few seconds, the children make their request again, taking advantage of the fact that 'now' can change its denotation over a discourse.

as (1), even assuming her model of context-sensitivity to be correct. But the situation is worse for the contextualist. If the model of context-sensitivity assumed by the contextualist is wrong, some of what contextualists say about the virtues of their theories over other theories is vitiated.

If different occurrences of instances of 'knows that p' can be associated with different epistemic standards within a discourse, some of the paradigm sentences the infelicity of which supposedly motivates their accounts over rival accounts turn out to be felicitous and potentially true by contextualist lights. For example, if we have similar behavior to many other context-sensitive expressions, one would expect the following to be felicitous:

(10) Bill knows that he has hands, but Bill does not know that he is not a bodiless brain in a vat.

(11) Bill does not know that he is not a bodiless brain in a vat, but Bill knows he has hands.

As we have seen above, DeRose takes the persistent infelicity of utterances of the sentences in (10) and (11) to undermine alternative accounts on the grounds that they allow for acceptable utterances of these sentences. But, if instances of 'knows that p' are context-sensitive, then one would expect there to be contexts in which the sentences in (10) and (11) could be felicitously uttered. Someone who uttered sentence (10) would intend 'knows that he has hands' to be associated with lower standards, and 'know that he is not a bodiless brain in a vat' to be associated with higher standards. Someone uttering sentence (11) would be lowering standards across a conjunction.

With other context-sensitive expressions, we do find constructions analogous to those in (10) and (11) that can be felicitously uttered. For instance, consider again:

(7) In Atlanta, there are many serial killers but not many unemployed men.

'Many' is analogous to the indexical contextualist's view that 'know' is itself a context-sensitive term, which denotes different relations relative to different contexts of use. But in (7), the two semantic values of 'many' are different, despite the fact that they occur within the same clause. The occurrence of the expression 'serial killer' leads us to interpret the first occurrence of 'many' in one way, whereas the occurrence of the expression 'unemployed men' leads us to interpret the second occurrence in another way. Similarly, if the contextualist were right, one might wonder why the occurrence of 'he has hands' should not lead us to interpret the relevant occurrences of 'know' in one way (as denoting low-standards knowledge relations), while the occurrence of 'he is not a bodiless brain in a vat' leads us to interpret the other occurrences of 'know' in (10) and (11) in another way (as denoting high-standards knowledge relations).

According to the versions of contextualism developed in Schaffer (2004) and Ludlow (2005), instances of the predicate 'know that p' are context-sensitive, because there is an epistemologically significant context-sensitive element associated with 'know' in the predicate (though the lexical item 'know' is not context-sensitive). But consider:

(12) That mountain is tall for Michigan, but not tall for Colorado.

In (12), we find that different occurrences of the same adjective can be associated with different values for their contextually sensitive parameters within the same clause. So we would expect different occurrences of 'know' to be able to be associated with distinct values for their associated contextually sensitive parameters within the same clause.

The contextualist might respond that the reason that (12) can be felicitously uttered is that we have devices that make explicit the comparison class properties for gradable adjectives, as in 'for Michigan' and 'for Colorado'. Perhaps the infelicity of uttering the sentences in (10) and (11) is due to the inability we have to articulate the shifting standards associated with our knowledge claims, and when we cannot articulate the shift, extralinguistic context cannot do the task of shifting the standards for us.

This line of enquiry does not advance the contextualist's cause very far. For if there is no way to articulate the changing standards, as there is in the case of comparison class properties for gradable adjectives (or quantifier domains for quantifiers), that should simply raise more worry about the contextualist's thesis that epistemic vocabulary is context-sensitive in the way she describes. For with other context-sensitive constructions, we do find ways to articulate what is sometimes provided by context. If the epistemic standards cannot be smoothly linguistically articulated, that should lead us to worry that they are not there.

A perhaps more promising path for the contextualist to pursue is the one urged by Peter Ludlow (2005). Ludlow calls attention in his paper to the presence of standards operators in epistemic talk, as in examples such as:

(13) John doesn't know that water is liquid by the standards of chemistry.
(14) Copernicus didn't know that the sun was the center of the solar system by today's standards of knowledge.

Ludlow takes expressions such as 'by the standards of chemistry' and 'by today's standards of knowledge' to play an analogous function to the expressions 'for Michigan' and 'for Colorado', which articulate comparison class properties. Such expressions make explicit the standard of knowledge relative to which an ascription of knowledge is true or false.

Contextualism is the thesis that knowledge ascriptions are context-sensitive in an epistemologically distinctive way. Ludlow takes the presence of expressions in English such as 'by the standards of chemistry' or 'by today's standards of knowledge' to show that *unembellished* knowledge ascriptions, ones that do not contain explicit standards operators, nevertheless contain an unpronounced position for epistemic standards. That is, Ludlow takes the existence of such expressions to show that, in a sentence such as 'John knows that he has hands', there is an unpronounced position in the verb phrase 'knows that he has hands' that, relative to a context, receives an epistemic standard as a value. That is how Ludlow proposes to derive contextualism from the felicity and potential truth of sentences such as (13) and (14).

Ludlow is indisputably correct in his observation that people regularly utter sentences such as (13) and (14). However, the phenomenon he discusses is not specifically epistemic in character. Expressions such as 'by loose standards', 'by strict standards', and 'by the standards of chemistry' regularly occur appended to sentences that contain no epistemic vocabulary at all (cf. Lewis 1981: 84):

(15) By strict standards, France is not hexagonal.
(16) By loose standards, this table is square.
(17) By the standards of chemistry, what is in the Hudson River isn't water.

Expressions such as 'by strict standards', 'by loose standards' and 'by the standards of chemistry' cannot be used to derive a conclusion about specifically epistemic context-sensitivity. The pattern of usage of these expressions is considerably more general in character. It has something to do with the phenomenon that is called *loose use*.

Even abstracting from the fact that (as I will argue in the next chapter) appeal to loose use is not of help to the contextualist, there are other objections to Ludlow's proposed inference. If Ludlow takes the felicity and potential truth of sentences such as (13) and (14) to license the postulation of epistemic standards variables in unembellished knowledge ascriptions, then, by parity of reasoning, he needs to take the felicity and potential truth of sentences such as (15)–(17) as licensing the postulation of various kinds of standards positions in sentences such as 'this is water', 'this is square', and 'this is hexagonal'. Indeed, there are more than just considerations from parity of reasoning at work here, since one can conjoin knowledge attributions and non-epistemic statements in the scope of expressions such as 'by the standards of chemistry', as in:

(18) By the standards of chemistry, what is in the Hudson River isn't water, and John doesn't know that water is liquid.

(19) By loose standards, this table is square and John knows that water is a liquid.

Since there is only one occurrence of a standards expression in (18) and (19), its effect on the embedded non-epistemic sentence must be the same as its effect on the epistemic sentence. If it binds a standards parameter in the epistemic sentence, it binds a standards parameter in the non-epistemic sentence. It follows that, if one takes the felicity and potential truth of (13) and (14) to license the postulation of epistemic standards variables, one would need standards positions in the syntax for *virtually every predication*. This is deeply implausible. Furthermore, the conclusion, even if it were plausible, is of no help to the theorist who wishes to establish that knowledge ascriptions have a specifically *epistemological* kind of context-sensitivity. So the contextualist should certainly reject Ludlow's position.[15]

---

[15] There are a number of other reasons to question the inference Ludlow draws. First, there are similar inferences that are clearly invalid (a 'bad-company' objection). From the truth of 'according to John, chocolate is made of gold', we cannot conclude that the unembellished sentence 'chocolate is made of gold' contains a reference to persons. It is similarly unclear what legitimates Ludlow's inference. More theoretically, on a very natural construal of these operators, they are adjuncts and not arguments. If so, they are only optionally present, and not present when phonologically unarticulated. In response, Ludlow rejects the argument–adjunct distinction. He argues that many expressions that we think of as adjuncts really mark positions that are linguistically active, even when unpronounced. Ludlow suggests e.g. that there is a position for an instrument (such as 'with a knife') in a sentence such as 'John cut the salami'. On this view, even when this position is not explicitly articulated (as it is in 'John cut the salami with a knife') its value may be contextually supplied. But there is no position for instruments in 'John cut the

Ludlow's view that knowledge ascriptions contain an implicit reference to standards cannot be pressed into service to rescue the contextualist from the charge that knowledge ascriptions behave quite differently from other context-sensitive expressions. Contextualists do in general claim that there are special rules governing the context-sensitivity of instances of 'know that p'. In particular, once a skeptical possibility has been raised, they say, that has ramifications for the evaluation of future uses of instances of 'know that p' within that discourse. But there are two worries for this strategy. First, it leaves the oddity of (10) unexplained. Secondly, as I have emphasized, it stipulates a certain pragmatic constraint about the context-sensitivity of instances of 'know that p' that has no parallel with pragmatic principles governing the interpretations of other context-sensitive expressions. Thus, these kinds of claims about how raising skeptical scenarios change the discourse look like stipulations to save the theory from having similar uncomfortable consequences as rival theories.

I have argued that the contextualist needs knowledge ascriptions to have very different properties from familiar context-sensitive constructions. These arguments leave open the possibility that the alleged context-sensitivity of instances of 'know that p' could be modeled on the context-sensitivity of some other kind of expression, one that does not allow for standard shifts within a clause, and is undetectable by the above tests involving propositional anaphora and assertion reports.[16]

---

salami' that can be contextually supplied (see Stanley (2005b)). If Bill utters 'John cut the salami with a knife', Frank can deny his assertion by uttering 'No he didn't; he cut it with a spoon'. But if Bill utters only 'John cut the salami', no matter what information is salient in extralinguistic context, it is never felicitous to follow his assertion with 'No he didn't; he cut it with a spoon'. So Ludlow's argument that 'with a knife' is present even when unpronounced fails.

[16] Barbara Partee (p.c.) pointed out to me that the relational term 'enemy' does not easily allow for shifts in interpretation within a clause. An utterance of the sentence 'John is an enemy and Bill is an enemy, but they are not enemies of the same person' is decidedly odd. Similarly, though one can switch from the

A complete case against the contextualist would involve canvassing every kind of context-sensitive expression, and showing some clear disanalogy between the behaviors of expressions of that kind and instances of 'know that p'. This is obviously a task that cannot be accomplished here. However, the above arguments are not thereby rendered idle. Before such a task is undertaken, one might think that there are surely some context-sensitive expressions that behave like knowledge ascriptions. But the above discussions show that there is no familiar kind of context-sensitivity upon which to base the alleged context-sensitivity of knowledge ascriptions. The burden of proof is therefore on the contextualist to produce one.

'can' of physical possibility to the 'can' of permissibility within a clause (as in 'John can lift the table that Mary says he can'), it is harder to switch the domain of modals such as 'can', fixing a sense of possibility. But I have provided other arguments to distinguish these expressions from knowledge ascriptions. The examples from propositional anaphora, and examples such as TECHNOLOGY, were so intended.

4

Contextualism on the Cheap?

In the previous two chapters, I have provided an argument against the contextualist's empirical claim that knowledge attributions are context-sensitive in a distinctively epistemological manner. The method I employed was to draw upon properties of all sorts of context-sensitive constructions, and argue that knowledge-ascriptions lack these properties. With the use of such arguments, one cannot conclusively demonstrate that knowledge ascriptions are not context-sensitive in the way the contextualist maintains. But the considerations of the previous two chapters do suggest that the only positive evidence there is for the contextualist's claim that knowledge ascriptions are context-sensitive is the fact that contextualism can provide an account of the cases described in the Introduction.

But there are some philosophers who believe there are more direct ways to show that a given construction is context-sensitive than by drawing an analogy between instances of 'know that *p*' and uncontroversial context-sensitive constructions. My aim in this chapter is to treat some of their arguments, which promise to justify contextualism about knowledge attributions 'on the cheap'.

Here is the first kind of argument I have in mind (due to Stewart Cohen (p.c.)). One might think that the verb 'hit' is context-sensitive, for the following reason. We can envisage a society in which people regularly have strong friendly physical contact. In this society, one has to strike someone with far more force to count as 'hitting' them than in our own society. So 'hit' is context-sensitive. And it is not much of a stretch to say that 'know' behaves similarly to 'hit'. After all, we can easily envisage a society in which people require someone to have non-question begging evidence that deductively entails p in order for the predicate 'knows that p' to be truly applied to them. If the former consideration shows 'hit' to be context-sensitive, then the latter consideration shows instances of 'knows that p' to be context-sensitive in the way that the contextualist contends.

However, this argument is fallacious. Just because there is a possible society that does not apply the word 'hit' to actions under the same conditions as we do does not show that the word 'hit' is context-sensitive. After all, there is a possible society that applies the expression 'even number' only to male donkeys. That certainly does not show that the expression 'even number' is context-sensitive. Nothing follows about the context-sensitivity of a construction by appeal to possible societies that use that construction with a different meaning from ours.

A similar point holds with appeals to explicit stipulations. One can envisage a group that stipulates that the word 'hit' is to apply only to actions that involve a certain level of force. Again, this does not show that the word 'hit' is context-sensitive. We can also imagine a group that stipulates that the word 'hit' is to apply only to actions that involve winking. Since the latter obviously does not show that 'hit' is context-sensitive, neither does the former.

The next argument is also due to Stewart Cohen. Cohen attempts to argue, from premises about the word 'justified', to conclusions about the word 'know'. Here is a short version of Cohen's argument (1999: 60), in his own words:

Does knowledge come in degrees? Most people say no (though David Lewis says yes). But it doesn't really matter. For, on my view, justification, or having good reasons, is a component of knowledge, and justification certainly comes in degrees. So context will determine how justified a belief must be in order to be justified simpliciter.

This suggests a further argument for the truth of the contextualist's claim about knowledge. Since justification is a component of knowledge, an ascription of knowledge involves an ascription of justification. And for the reasons just indicated, ascriptions of justification are context-sensitive.

Cohen's argument for the context-sensitivity of 'know' has roughly the following structure:

COHEN

Premise 1. Gradable adjectives are context-sensitive.

Premise 2. So, we can expect the gradable adjective 'justified' to be context-sensitive.

Premise 3. 'S knows P' means in part what is meant by 'P is justified for S'.

Conclusion. So the truth of 'S knows P' depends upon context.

Before I evaluate Cohen's argument, I want to note that Cohen is not entitled both to the soundness of his argument, and to neutrality on the gradability of instances of 'knows that *p*'. For if this argument is sound, then surely so is:

COHEN*

Premise 1. Gradable adjectives are sensitive to contextually salient scales.

Premise 2. So, we can expect the gradable adjective 'justified' to be sensitive to contextually salient scales.

Premise 3. 'S knows P' means in part what is meant by 'P is justified for S'.

Conclusion. So the truth of 'S knows P' is sensitive to contextually salient scales.

So it seems that Cohen's argument may commit the contextualist to the gradability of instances of 'knows that *p*'.

However, a more pressing task is to evaluate the soundness of Cohen's argument from the gradability of 'justified' to the conclusion that 'know' is context-sensitive. The word 'justified' is a gradable adjective. We may say 'My belief that Bush is conservative is more justified than my belief that Kerry is liberal'. It does not, however, follow that 'justified' is context-sensitive. Some expressions are gradable, yet not context-sensitive. Consider, for example, the expression 'taller than 6 feet'. This expression is clearly not context-sensitive. But it is gradable; we may speak of someone being *much* taller than 6 feet. So the expression 'taller than 6 feet' is gradable, but not context-sensitive. So gradability does not entail context-sensitivity.

The point that gradability does not entail context-sensitivity can be made more theoretically. The gradability of an expression is due to the fact that the expression is semantically linked to a scale. Something is more or less F depending upon its position on the scale associated with F. But an expression can be semantically linked with a scale, even though there is a designated point on that scale that, for any context *c*, is the point of demarcation between F and not-F. This is what we see with expressions such as 'taller than 6 feet'. Something can be much taller than 6 feet, even though it is a context-independent matter whether or not something is taller than 6 feet.

So, the conclusion that 'justified' is context-sensitive does not follow from the premise that it is gradable. My own view is that 'justified' is gradable but not context-sensitive, much like 'taller than 6 feet'. For a belief to be justified means for it to be justified over the context-invariant degree of justification, just as to be taller than 6 feet is to be taller than the context-invariant degree of a height of 6 feet. So I do not accept the first two premises of COHEN.

Despite the fact that I do not accept the first two premises of COHEN, I think it is important to emphasize that the argument would not be sound, even if the first two premises were true. For, if Premise 3 is construed in such a way as to make its truth fairly uncontroversial, the argument is not valid.

The claim accepted by most epistemologists is that, in the analysis of the knowledge relation, some justification property appears. That is:

The Knowledge-Justification Thesis
Some justification property is part of the conceptual analysis of the knowledge relation.

The Knowledge-Justification Thesis is an informal way of making explicit the thesis that knowledge is analyzed in terms of justification.[1]

However, if Premise 3 is another way of stating the Knowledge-Justification Thesis, then COHEN is not valid. For the Knowledge-Justification Thesis is not a claim about a relation between the word 'know' and the word 'justified'. It is rather the claim about the relation between the knowledge relation and some justification property. From such a claim, together with the thesis (which I am granting for the sake of argument) that the *word* 'justified' is context-sensitive, nothing follows about the context-sensitivity of the word 'know'.

One might think that there is a prima facie case to be made, from the fact that a certain term t contains in the analysis of what it expresses a property that is expressed by a context-sensitive term t', that t is therefore context-sensitive. But this is not true. Consider the term 'vacuum'. A plausible analysis of the notion of being a vacuum involves being completely empty. But the property of being empty is expressed by the context-sensitive word 'empty'. This does not entail that 'vacuum' is context-sensitive.[2]

---

[1] The Knowledge-Justification Thesis, as I have formulated it, construes conceptual analysis as a metaphysical project concerned with exploring the constituent parts of properties; for more on this topic, see King (1998).

[2] Of course it is true that 'vacuum', like all words, can be used loosely. This is of no use to the contextualism, as I will argue below.

Another example is the expression 'John's enemy'. There is at least a prima facie case that this expression is not context-sensitive.[3] But analyzing the notion of being John's enemy involves appealing to the notion of being an enemy, which is expressed by the context-sensitive word 'enemy' (in one context, it may mean an enemy of x, and, in another context, an enemy of y).

So, if Premise 3 is supposed to reflect the Knowledge-Justification Thesis, it does not allow Cohen to draw the conclusion that instances of 'know that p' are context-sensitive in a distinctively epistemological way. But one might think that, intuitively, an attribution of knowledge entails an attribution of justification. Evidence for this is that it is odd to utter instances of 'x knows that p, but x is not justified in believing that p.' In other words, there is good evidence for the following thesis:

The Metalinguistic Entailment Thesis
For any context c, if what is expressed in c by a sentence of the form 'x knows that p' is true, then what is expressed in c by a sentence for the form 'x is justified in believing that p' is true.

Perhaps Premises 1 and 2 of COHEN, together with the Metalinguistic Entailment Thesis, will provide a valid argument for the conclusion that knowledge attributions are context-sensitive.

Unfortunately for the contextualist, the Metalinguistic Entailment Thesis, together with Premises 1 and 2 of COHEN, does not entail that knowledge attributions are context-sensitive. For it may be that knowledge entails the highest kind of justification. For example, suppose that 'is justified' is context-dependent, but that the most demanding property denoted by 'is justified',

---

[3] When a possessive is used with a relational noun such as 'enemy', it forces a reading in which the possession relation is determined by the nature of the noun (e.g. 'John's brother'). There are uses of such constructions in which the possession relation can be assigned a different reading (suppose John is one of a group of police officers each of whom is interviewing one of the four brothers of the suspect in a crime). But it is not clear that such cases are genuine readings of the possessive, rather than deferred reference of some kind.

relative to any context, is one such that knowing a proposition requires standing in that most demanding justification relation to that proposition. This position respects the truth of the Metalinguistic Entailment Thesis. Yet it is also consistent with the thesis that knowledge attributions are not context-sensitive, while justification attributions are context-sensitive. Furthermore, the position is not tantamount to skepticism. For it could be that the highest level of justification ever denoted by 'is justified' is not particularly high. So the fact that a knowledge attribution seems to entail a justification attribution, even coupled with the claim that justification attributions are context-sensitive, does not entail that knowledge attributions are context-sensitive.

The thesis Cohen requires to move from the context-sensitivity of 'justified' to the context-sensitivity of 'know' is rather the following:

The Metalinguistic Containment Thesis
For any context c, the word 'know' expresses a relation that, relative to that context, contains as a component the property expressed by the word 'justified', relative to c.

Suppose that one stands in the relation expressed by 'know', relative to a context of use, to a proposition p, if and only if one truly believes that p, and bears some justification relation to that proposition. Suppose further that 'is justified' is context-sensitive, and the Metalinguistic Containment Thesis is true. Then it does follow that the content of the word 'know' changes across contexts, in parallel with the content of the word 'justified'.

However, it is quite unclear how to argue for the Metalinguistic Containment Thesis. In particular, it is not clear how to provide an argument for the Metalinguistic Containment Thesis that is not more plausibly accommodated by assuming the truth of the weaker Metalinguistic Entailment Thesis, which is, as we have seen, of no help to the contextualist. For example, one cannot support the Metalinguistic Containment Thesis by appeal to the oddity of uttering instances of the schema 'X knows that p, but X isn't justified in believing that p'. The oddity of utterances of instances of that schema provides evidence only for the weaker Metalinguistic Entailment Thesis, which is fully consistent with the falsity of contextualism about knowledge attributions. Since it is not at all obvious how to argue for the Metalinguistic Containment Thesis, there is no persuasive route from the fact that 'justified' is a gradable adjective to the context-sensitivity of 'know'.

The third way to argue for contextualism 'on the cheap' is to appeal to *ambiguity* or *loose use*. Contextualists such as Cohen, DeRose, and Lewis have, to their credit, not presented their views in these terms. There is really not much to be said for a version of contextualism according to which 'know' is ambiguous. To ground an ambiguity claim linguistically, one would need to show that there are languages in which the different meanings are represented by different words. But such a claim is unlikely to be substantiated in the cases of interest to the contextualist. It is quite unlikely that there are languages in which the word for 'know' in the epistemology classroom is different from the word for 'know' outside the epistemology classroom.

The more interesting case involves *loose use*. Suppose a contextualist were to present her claims in these terms. Then, on this view, when 'standards are low', one is using 'know' loosely, and this is why it is acceptable to predicate a knowledge state of someone who has only weak inductive evidence for the truth of one of her (true) beliefs. When 'standards are high', then 'know' is used strictly, and it is not acceptable to attribute knowledge to that person in that situation.

Here are some typical cases of loose use. One may utter 'France is hexagonal', to describe the rough shape of France. Though intuitively France is not 'strictly' hexagonal, such an utterance can be felicitously made. Similarly, suppose someone utters 'It's 3 o'clock' when asked the time at 3:03. Her response can be felicitous, even though it is not intuitively 'strictly' true. Finally, suppose that in a village there is a person Mary with a small amount of medical training, and no one else has any medical training at all. In context, it may be appropriate to utter 'Mary is the doctor of the village', though it is intuitively not strictly true. These are all cases in which, intuitively, language is used 'loosely'.[4]

There are two kinds of accounts one could envisage of such cases. According to the first, and by far the most natural, utterances of such sentences express propositions that are literally false, but the utterances are nevertheless pragmatically acceptable. On the second account, utterances of such sentences express propositions that are literally true.

Suppose the contextualist took the first account, according to which loose use involved the expression of literally false propositions despite pragmatic felicity. On such an account, ordinary knowledge attributions that are generally held to be true would be pragmatically felicitous, but would express false propositions. Only when someone satisfies strict epistemological standards could an atomic knowledge attribution to that person be true. On this view, we generally speak falsely when we attribute knowledge to our fellow epistemic citizens, though we are not thereby violating conversational norms.

But this is obviously an unsatisfactory position way to present the contextualist view. For this position is simply *epistemological skepticism*. Ordinary knowledge attributions are generally false. But skepticism was precisely the view that the contextualist position was supposed to help us evade. Therefore, the contextualist position cannot be presented as the view that knowledge ascriptions are used loosely, where loose use is understood on the pragmatic model.

Therefore, if contextualism about knowledge attributions is supposed to be understood on the model of loose use, then its proponents must have a semantic account of loose use. I do not

---

[4] My own suspicion is that there is no uniform phenomenon behind 'loose use'.

pretend to understand what would motivate a semantic account of loose use. After all, the common feature to cases of loose use is that they seem to be cases in which it is felicitous to describe something as satisfying a predicate, despite the fact that the thing in question does not satisfy the predicate, when it is taken literally. A semantic account of loose use is prima facie odd, since one might think that, in order for something to satisfy a predicate semantically, it must at least satisfy the literal meaning of that predicate. To attempt to capture loose use semantically seems therefore to miss the phenomenon being described.

Be that as it may, suppose one adopted a semantic account of loose use, and couched contextualism about 'know' as the thesis that 'know', like paradigm cases of loose use, can be used loosely. Then an ordinary atomic knowledge attribution to someone with only weak inductive evidence for one of her true beliefs can express a true proposition, because it is used loosely, and loose talk is a semantic, rather than a solely pragmatic phenomenon.

But what would it mean to present contextualism along the lines of a semantic account of loose use? It is not sufficient to say that a semantic account of loose use is one according to which 'know' expresses different properties in different contexts. For this is true of any context-dependent account. Constructions involving gradable adjectives such as 'tall' or 'flat' involve some expression having different contents in different contexts, but this does not mean that they are best modeled by appeal to 'loose use'. It is not that 'tall' is being used loosely, as in the paradigm cases above, when an 8-year-old child who is 5 feet tall is described as 'tall'. It is rather that 'tall' (or some expression associated with it) can have different contents in different contexts, consistent with it being used perfectly literally. A contextualist theory of knowledge attributions modeled along the lines of loose use (construed semantically) is therefore not just a view according to which knowledge attributions can change their contents across contexts. It must rather flow from some rather tight analogy between paradigm cases of loose use and knowledge attributions. On this account, it is because knowledge attributions in ordinary contexts are *like* uttering at 3:03 p.m. the sentence 'It is 3 o'clock' that they can be truthfully asserted. The point of the analogy between knowledge attributions and loose talk would then be to free the contextualist from having to relate knowledge attributions to constructions such as comparative adjectives and other context-sensitive constructions that (unlike 'know') are gradable or can engage in sentence-internal context shifts.

So, a contextualist 'loose-talk' account of knowledge is one according to which knowledge attributions are context-sensitive 'in the same sense' as it is permissible to describe 3:03 p.m. as satisfying the predicate 'is 3 o'clock', and France as satisfying the predicate 'is hexagonal'. But now it seems that this version of contextualism would face a similar charge to the pragmatic loose-talk version of contextualism. According to this version of contextualism, Hannah can satisfy the predicate 'knows that she has hands' only in the sense that France can satisfy the predicate 'is hexagonal', 3:03 p.m. can satisfy the predicate 'is 3 o'clock', and someone with rudimentary medical training can satisfy the predicate 'is a doctor'. This is not a very satisfying way of 'rescuing' ordinary knowledge attributions. Indeed, one may wonder whether it has any advantages over skepticism at all.

So, contextualists have in general been correct not to employ either the ambiguity or the 'loose-talk' versions of their theses. The former seems subject to empirical refutation, and the latter seems no different from the skeptical positions they rightly reject.

Given the paucity of the linguistic evidence for contextualism, and the lack of an alternative way to establish it, the evidence for contextualism rests solely upon the cases discussed in the Introduction. If there were a non-contextualist explanation of these intuitions, however, then that would provide a significant blow to contextualism, for then the last remaining piece of evidence in support of contextualism would be removed. It is to this task that I now turn.

5

Interest-Relative Invariantism

Bare Interest-Relative Invariantism (henceforth IRI) is simply the claim that whether or not someone knows that *p* may be determined in part by practical facts about the subject's environment. So, like contextualism, IRI is consistent with a number of different theories of the knowledge relation(s). The advocate of IRI simply proposes that, in addition to whatever one's favored theory of knowledge says about when *x* knows at time *t* that *p*, there is a further condition on knowledge that has to do with practical facts about the subject's environment. One could, therefore, combine IRI with any number of widely differing views about the nature of the knowledge relation.

For example, according to *probabilistic strength of evidence* IRI, practical facts about a subject's environment at time *t* might make it the case that that subject must have stronger evidence than usual in order to know a proposition *p* at that time than she must possess in order to know that proposition at other times, where strength of evidence is measured in probabilistic terms. According to *relevant alternatives* IRI, practical facts about a subject's environment at time *t* might make it the case that, in order to know a certain proposition p at that time, that subject must rule out a different set of alternative propositions than she has to rule out at another time t'. And so on. What makes all of these different theories instances of IRI is that all of them include an additional condition on knowledge, one that involves practical facts about the subject's situation at the putative time of knowing.

It is an uncontroversial linguistic thesis that verbs are associated with temporal variables, the value of which, relative to a context, is the time at which the verb's application is said to occur.[1] So a knowledge ascription is really of the form 'x knows at t that p'. According to the advocate of IRI, the only context-sensitivity that is associated with knowledge ascriptions involves the assignment of a time to the temporal variable associated with the verb, and the resolution of all non-epistemically relevant context-sensitive expressions in the knowledge ascription. So according to the advocate of IRI, a knowledge ascription such as 'Herman knows at 1:30 p.m. on September 24, 2004 that Hillary Clinton is a Democrat' expresses the same proposition relative to every context of use, and hence is not context-sensitive.[2] There is no specifically epistemic sense in which knowledge attributions are context-sensitive. IRI is therefore not a version of contextualism. According to IRI, there is a univocal knowledge relation, which is sensitive to the subject's practical situation at the putative time of knowing.

It is worth expanding upon why an interest-relative invariantist account is so readily available in the case of knowledge, but not in some other cases (we return to this topic in detail in the final chapter). Contextualism has been advanced as a reply to a number of philosophical paradoxes. We are concerned here

---

[1] Linguists now reject the Priorian view that tenses are operators (see King 2003, and Chapter 7 below).

[2] I am assuming here that orthographically similar names that have different semantic values are occurrences of different expressions (just as there may be two Hillary Clintons, so there may be two 'Hillary Clintons').

with contextualism as a response to the skeptical paradoxes, and therefore with contextualism about instances of 'knows that p'. But contextualism has also been advanced as a reply to the liar paradox (contextualism about 'true') and as a reply to the sorites paradox (contextualism about vague terms). But Interest-Relative Invariantist accounts are nowhere near as plausible in these other cases.

An ascription of truth is a sentence of the form 'S is true', where S is replaceable by names of sentences (or perhaps utterances or propositions). Contextualism about ascriptions of truth is that, as one makes different ascriptions of truth, the extension of the predicate 'true' can change across a discourse. This doctrine has proven useful in addressing the liar paradox. But it is, to say the least, difficult to see how to replace contextualism about 'true' with an interest-relative invariantist account of truth. It is not clear that the predicate 'is true' is associated with a temporal variable. And the subject of the ascription of truth is a sentence (or utterance or proposition). It is just unclear how to construct a version of IRI with these resources. Finally, even if one could find a way to justify inclusion of interests into an ascription of truth, it is unclear how this would help with the liar paradox. After all, the liar paradox is generated by appeal to the disquotation principle governing the truth predicate. Context-sensitivity provides a way of undermining the disquotation principle, but interest-relativity does not.

With knowledge ascriptions, in contrast, the subject of the knowledge ascription and the time of the knowing are both specified by constituents of the proposition expressed by the knowledge ascription. So one can characterize the conditions under which someone stands in the knowledge relation to a proposition at a time in terms of the arguments of the knowledge relation. No appeal to the context of use of the sentence is necessary in order to specify the practical facts about the subject of the knowledge ascription that are relevant for whether the subject knows the proposition in question. So IRI is an option that does not involve revision of any standard linguistic commitments, or adoption of any version of contextualism.

IRI is the claim that knowledge is sensitive to an additional traditionally non-epistemic factor. Since the advocate of IRI can marry this claim with a number of distinct theories of knowledge, explicitness about the details of the theory of knowledge that one prefers will distract our attention from the point of IRI. For the sake of explicitness, however, it is worth considering an interest-relative invariantist version of a traditional epistemological theory.

The theory I will consider is one according to which knowing a true proposition requires a subject who believes it to possess a sufficient level of evidence for that proposition, where sufficiency is measured in terms of some kind of probability. The basic idea is that, the greater the practical investment one has in a belief, the stronger one's evidence must be in order to know it, where strength of evidence is modeled probabilistically.

There are numerous problems with the approach I will take, and it is worthwhile being clear about these problems at the outset. First, exploiting probability in any analysis of knowledge (or any other epistemic notion) will require a notion of *epistemic* probability (rather than some more objective notion) in whose analysis the epistemic notion being analyzed will certainly re-occur. That is, knowledge might be a more basic notion than any notion of epistemic probability used in its 'analysis' (see Williamson 2000). Secondly, there are problem cases, such as Lottery propositions, that suggest that any analysis in terms of probability is doomed to failure (though an interest-relative invariantist version of this theory can smooth out some of these problems, see Hawthorne (2004: 160 ff.)). Thirdly, the theory I develop appears to distinguish evidence from knowledge in an implausible way. More specifically, it appears on the account I give that the only epistemic notion interest-relativity affects is knowledge, by requiring subjects occasionally to have more evidence. But if knowledge is an interest relative notion, it is likely that other epistemic notions that are intimately intertwined with it, such as evidence and justification, will also be similarly interest-relative.[3]

I am not sanguine about the possibility of providing an analysis of knowledge, and that is not my interest here. Rather, my purpose is to establish that knowledge is conceptually connected to practical interests. This point is compatible with many different approaches to the nature of knowledge. For the sake of perspicuity, it helps to choose a particular first-order account of knowledge, and show how adding the relevant connections to practical interests allows us to capture facts about knowledge that we would otherwise not be in a position to explain. But all first-order theories of knowledge are problematic. So choosing any such theory will raise the problems specific to it. But since I am choosing one particular first-order theory just for purposes of illustration, in order to show how it is affected by the addition of the conceptual connection to practical interests, the problems with the first-order theory I choose are not problems for my project. So we may as well choose this one to develop along interest-relative invariantist lines, bearing in mind the limitations of any attempted account of knowledge in terms of probability of any kind.

Here is one way to develop the view I am considering (x, w, t, and p are schematic letters replaceable by names of persons, worlds, times, and propositions respectively):

Knows ($<x, w, t, p>$) if and only if (1) p is true at w (2) $\sim p$ is not a serious epistemic possibility for x at w and t (3) If p is a serious practical question for x at t, then $\sim p$ has a sufficiently low epistemic probability, given x's total evidence (4) x believes at t that p on the basis of non-inferential evidence, or believes that

---

[3] This latter worry is mitigated somewhat by the response to the first worry. Since one would need to appeal to knowledge to spell out the notion of epistemic probability, the interest-relativity of knowledge may after all transfer to the interest-relativity of the relevant notion of evidence.

p on the basis of a competent inference from propositions that are known by x at t.

This thesis about knowledge contains several notions that require elucidation. First, there are the notions of evidence and probability. Secondly, I must explain the notions of a serious epistemic possibility and that of a serious practical question. Before explaining these notions, it is useful to contrast this semantic clause with a contextualist account.

A sentence is context-sensitive if and only if it expresses different propositions in different contexts of use. There is a relatively trivial sense in which the above semantic clause is part of a contextualist semantics for knowledge attributions. As is standard, I assume that knowledge attributions, like other sentences, express propositions about particular times. One and the same knowledge attribution may express different propositions at different times, because the temporal element in the knowledge attribution is assigned different times in different contexts of use. So, knowledge attributions are context-sensitive, on my view, in the sense that different knowledge attributions are about different times. But this is a relatively innocuous sense of contextualism; it is true of all verbs that they are associated with temporal elements that receive different values at different times. On the semantic clause I have just given, there is no specifically *epistemological* sense in which knowledge attributions are context-sensitive.

For example, on this account, there is no semantic context-sensitivity associated with the word 'know'. The word 'know' expresses the same relation in every context—namely, the one described in the above clause. Furthermore, whether or not a proposition is a serious epistemic possibility or a serious practical alternative is determined by facts about the subject of the knowledge attribution and the time of knowing. So the facts about knowledge are not crucially dependent on the context in which the knowledge attribution is made (except insofar as these facts determine the value of the temporal index associated with 'know'—i.e. the time of knowing). So there is only a relatively trivial sense in which the semantics is a contextualist one.

Here is a brief explanation of the notions of evidence and probability to which I am appealing in the above account. I take the evidence an agent has to be a set of propositions and perhaps non-propositional experiential elements, to which that agent bears a privileged epistemic relation. Above, I speak of *the epistemic probability of a proposition relative to the total evidence of an agent*, a notion to which I also appeal below, in the characterization of serious epistemic possibility. By calling this notion epistemic, I mean to contrast it with subjective notions of probability, as well as more objective conceptions of probability, such as those involving the frequency in which an event would occur, given the truth of (or existence of) the evidence.[4] Since my interest is not in giving an account of knowledge in probabilistic terms, but rather with IRI, I will appeal to the placeholder notion of epistemic probability for my purposes.

Now I want to turn to a brief explanation of the notion of *serious epistemic possibility.* I take there to be a vague though relatively situation-invariant level of objective or epistemic probability that is relevant for determining serious epistemic possibility. For example, propositions that have an objective (or epistemic) probability of 50 percent or over, given a subject's total evidence, certainly count as meeting this level, and so are serious epistemic possibilities. I am not sure what more needs to be said about this vague but situation-invariant threshold level of probability.

So far, I have just appealed to an account of knowledge according to which knowing a true proposition one believes is a matter of having good evidence for it (where 'good' is explained in terms of some notion of probability). The way that IRI enters

---

[4] If we conceive of objective probability in terms of frequency, then having a high objective probability for a belief, given one's evidence, is very similar to having a reliable process giving rise to that belief.

into this so far familiar account of knowledge is via the notion of a serious practical question, and this is where our attention will be focused. If what is at issue in a given knowledge ascription is a proposition that is a serious practical question for the subject of the ascription at the time of the putative knowing, then the subject must have evidence that reduces the probability of the negation of this proposition to a sufficiently low level, where what is sufficiently low is determined by the costs of being wrong. The difficult question, however, is explaining what it is for a proposition to be a serious practical question for a subject at a time.

Under certain conditions, in decision making, a subject ought rationally to consider alternatives to propositions she believes. A subject's interests determine her goals. Given these goals, there will be a range of actions which that subject ought practically to consider.[5] Given that we are not ideal rational agents, there will be a range of alternatives that it will be legitimate to ignore. The rest of the alternatives to her beliefs are ones that she ought rationally to consider. A proposition is a serious practical question for an agent, if there are alternatives to that proposition that the subject ought rationally to consider in decision making.

Given that we are not ideal rational agents, what propositions is it legitimate to ignore in decision making? This is a serious problem in the theory of decision, one that I cannot hope to address satisfactorily here. My central claim is that there is such a notion, and that it has significance for both practical and theoretical rationality.

---

[5] As James Joyce (2002: 90) writes: 'H is a serious practical possibility for DM iff she is rationally required to factor the possibility of H's truth into her decision making.' I have used the phrase 'serious practical question' rather than 'serious practical possibility', because a proposition may be actually true, yet not a serious practical question—saying that the proposition is not a practical possibility is odd, because, on any legitimate notion of possibility, actual truth entails possible truth.

Though I cannot give a satisfactory account of the notion of a proposition that it is legitimate to ignore in decision making, there are some suggestive examples. Suppose that there is a 30 percent chance that Christine Todd Whitman will cut her toenails on September 1, 2003. On September 1, 2003, I am in my office, wondering whether to work on this chapter or work on a referee's report. Intuitively, the proposition that Christine Todd Whitman cuts her toenails on September 1, 2003 is not one that I need to take account of in my plans on September 1, 2003. It is one that I can legitimately ignore in my decision making, despite its relatively high possibility.

Here is another example. Consider the possibility that a large asteroid will hit the earth next week. If I were to discover this, this would have some effect on my plans. I would perhaps choose not to put off apologizing to my brother, and I may decide to shelve my plan to go on a diet. But, intuitively, it is still not a possibility that I need to take account of in my decision making.

As I have said, I have no general account of when it is that a possibility is not one I need to take account of in decision making. But the last example suggests three reasons why a proposition may be legitimately ignored. First, there might be a relatively small objective probability of it occurring, given my evidence. Secondly, there may be nothing I can do about whether or not it will occur. Thirdly, the actions I would take if I knew it would occur would not result in a substantial improvement in my life over the plan of action I already intended to pursue. All three of these features are present in the asteroid example.

It may be that a certain proposition is not a serious practical question for someone, but a consequence he or she may draw from it *is* a serious practical question (whether this is possible depends on the characterization of a serious practical question). In such cases, it may turn out that the negation of the consequence the agent draws has a sufficiently high probability, given the agent's interests and epistemic situation, to undermine the agent's knowledge of the consequence. If so, then the consequence is not known by that agent, even though it has been competently deduced by the agent from something known. But if this is possible, then x may competently deduce a proposition from something x knows, yet fail to know the proposition thereby deduced. That is, the worry here is that we may have a failure of what Timothy Williamson (2000: 117) has called *intuitive closure*.

I have no proof of the validity of intuitive closure, on the theory of knowledge I have given. But it is not obvious that it will license failures of intuitive closure. Suppose that p is not a serious practical question for x at t. But then, at t', x infers a consequence q from p, and q is (or thereby becomes) a serious practical question for x at t', according to the above characterization. Realizing that q follows from p would then change x's goals and interests. If so, then p becomes a serious practical question for x at t'. This may result in undermining x's knowledge of p at t'. So competently inferring a conclusion is in fact a way not only of *gaining* knowledge, but also of *undermining* knowledge.[6]

The notion of a serious practical question, a proposition that one must take into account in decision making, is highly intuitive. But I am not in possession of a satisfactory account of it. One possible avenue of exploration that addresses some of the above examples appeals to some notion of *warranted expected utility*. If whether or not a proposition is true has no effect (or only a minimal effect) on the warranted expected utilities of the actions at one's disposal, then it is not a serious practical question whether or not that proposition is true. That is, on this account, a proposition p is practically irrelevant if and only if, where $a_1 \ldots a_n$ are the actions at my disposal, the differences between the warranted expected utilities of $a_1 \ldots a_n$ relative to the nearest states of the world in which p are not meaningfully different from

---

[6] Harman and Sherman (2004) also suggest, albeit for different reasons, that competently inferring a conclusion from some premises may occasionally lead to undermining one's knowledge of the premises.

the differences between the warranted expected utilities of a_1 to a_n relative to the nearest states of the world in which $\sim p$.[7]

I have characterized this account in terms of the *warranted* expected utilities of the actions at an agent's disposal, because the agent might not be aware of what is in her own best interest, though, if she had some additional information, she would be. So the expected utility calculation, on this account, should be thought of as pertaining to the agent's warranted expected utilities, and not her subjective credences. But warranted expected utility is probably not sufficiently impersonal of a notion to do the required work. There may be facts relevant to the utility calculation that the agent is not epistemically responsible for knowing. So a more impersonal notion of utility may be required to capture the notion of a serious practical question. But I will speak in terms of warranted expected utility for the sake of clarity, bearing in mind that it is somewhat of a placeholder notion.

This account elegantly explains some of the above examples. For example, whether or not Christine Todd Whitman cut her toenails on September 1, 2003 has no effect on the expected utilities of the actions at my disposal. A similar explanation works for the other examples we considered. Another account of practical relevance that has some success with these paradigm examples has been suggested to me by Christian List (p.c.). On this account, a proposition p is practically relevant if and only if its truth or falsity would affect the *preference ordering* of the actions at my disposal. Clearly, whether or not Christine Todd Whitman cut her toenails has no effect on the preference ordering of the actions at my disposal. So, on this account of practical relevance, the proposition that Christine Todd Whitman cut her toenails is not a serious practical question. Though I prefer the first of these characterizations,

---

[7] This account cannot be quite correct, since knowing whether a certain proposition is true might affect which actions are at your disposal, without affecting the relevant warranted expect utility calculation.

I will not further defend it. The key idea, and one shared by any account of this form, is that what is of practical relevance can be of epistemic significance.

This account of knowledge needs to appeal to serious epistemic possibility, in addition to the notion of a serious practical question. Consider the proposition that you have an even number of hairs. I do not care how many hairs you have, but I believe that you have an even number of hairs. If you turned out to have an odd number of hairs, that would make no difference to me at all. The various options at my disposal are to retain my belief that you have an even number of hairs or give it up. Given that I do not care about the number of hairs you have, whether or not you have an odd number of hairs will not make a difference to the warranted expected utilities of retaining or discarding my belief. So, the proposition that you have an odd number of hairs is not a serious practical question for me. Nevertheless, it is epistemically relevant to my belief that you have an even number of hairs, because it is a serious possibility in the epistemic sense that you have an odd number of hairs.

The fact that the negation of a proposition is an epistemic possibility for an agent in a situation prevents the subject from knowing that proposition in that situation. However, the fact that a proposition is a serious practical question for an agent at a time does not automatically undermine that agent's knowledge of that proposition. It would only undermine the subject's knowledge of a proposition if, given her evidence, the probability of the negation of that proposition is not sufficiently low. A proposition might be a serious practical question, but its negation might have a sufficiently low likelihood, given the subject's evidence.

Now that we have sketched a 'strength of evidence' version of IRI, we may apply it to the examples introduced in the Introduction. In Low Stakes, the proposition that the bank is open on Saturday is not a serious practical question for Hannah. So we may suppose that Hannah's evidence is sufficient to justify her belief that she knows that the bank will be open on Saturday. In High Stakes, the proposition that the bank is open on Saturday is a serious practical question for Hannah, since, if it is not open, that will have a serious effect on the utility of some of the actions at her disposal (for example, going to the bank on Saturday instead of Friday). Since the proposition that the bank is open on Saturday is a serious practical question for Hannah, she does not have enough evidence to know it. This also explains why Jill's assertion, in Low Attributor–High Subject Stakes, of 'Hannah knows that the bank is open on Saturday, since she was there two weeks ago' is false. Since the proposition that the bank is open on Saturday is a serious practical question for Hannah, and she does not have enough evidence for it, Hannah does not know that the bank is open on Saturday. The same explanation is also available for why Hannah does not know that the bank is open in Ignorant High Stakes, despite her confidence. Since she *ought* to be aware of her impending bill, the fact that she has an impending bill is relevant for the warranted expected utility calculation. Since there is a potential negative cost on the utility of some of the actions she is considering, she does not know that the bank will be open on Saturday.

The case that IRI has the most difficulty with is High Attributor–Low Subject Stakes. In this situation, the stakes for Hannah are high. But the stakes for Bill are not high. So IRI predicts that Bill does know that the bank will be open on Saturday, though Hannah does not. This contradicts our intuition that Hannah's utterance of 'Bill doesn't know that the bank will be open' expresses a true proposition.

The fact that IRI gives a charitable explanation for all intuitions except for High Attributor–Low Subject Stakes is not a prima facie concern for the interest-relative invariantist. Recall that these intuitions are not intended simply to be data for an epistemological theory, as the grammaticality of various sentences may be taken to be data for a syntactic theory. Rather, the role of my appeal to our intuitions about these particular cases is to make vivid our commitment to the conceptual connection between knowledge and practical reasoning. From this perspective, the fact that we have the intuitions we do about High Attributor–Low Subject Stakes is mysterious. After all, it would be a mistake to allow idiosyncratic facts about my own practical situation to impinge upon my judgments about the practical rationality of someone in a quite different situation. So, unlike the intuitions we have about all of the other cases, the intuition we in fact have about High Attributor–Low Subject Stakes is not explicable by our commitment to the general theoretical principle that explains our intuitions in the other cases—namely, that one ought to act only upon what one knows. Given the intuitive connections between knowledge and practical reasoning, we should therefore be deeply suspicious of a theory that gives undue weight to our intuitions about High Attributor–Low Subject Stakes.

So I do not think that it is a point in favor of a theory that it gives a charitable explanation of our intuitions in High Attributor–Low Subject Stakes. However, the fact remains that we do have certain intuitions about cases like High Attributor–Low Subject Stakes, and this fact demands some kind of explanation, no matter what one's theory. One response to this dilemma for IRI, advocated by Hawthorne (2004: 160), is as follows. In order to assert that p, one must know that p. Because this is a general conversational maxim governing assertion, asserting that p implicates that one knows that p. Hannah is aware that it is very important for her that the bank is open on Saturday. So she is aware that she needs additional evidence in order to know that the bank will be open. So she cannot reasonably take herself to know that the bank will be open. But, if Bill knows that the bank will be open on Saturday, then the bank will be open on Saturday (since knowledge is factive). Since asserting that Bill knows that the bank will be open on Saturday will require her to know that Bill knows that the bank will be open on Saturday, and hence will require her to know that the bank will be open on Saturday,

Hannah cannot assert that Bill knows that the bank will be open on Saturday.

Hawthorne can successfully account for Hannah's failure to assert that Bill knows that the bank will be open on Saturday. But unfortunately Hawthorne does not successfully explain why Hannah *can* assert that Smith does *not* know that the bank will be open. Just because a proposition is not assertible does not mean that its negation is assertible; if I have no good evidence for or against *p*, *p* is not assertible, but neither is not-*p*. So Hawthorne's account does not explain why Hannah can assert that Bill does not know that the bank will be open on Saturday.

Here is a similar worry with Hawthorne's defense of IRI. The purported explanation of why the negation of the knowledge attribution is assertible is that to assert the knowledge attribution 'Bill knows that the bank will be open on Saturday' would implicate something false—namely, that Hannah reasonably takes herself to know that the bank will be open on Saturday. But it is not generally the case that 'not-*S*' is assertible if asserting *S* would implicate something false. To give an example, suppose that Frank believes Peter is a good philosopher. When asked by a department chair whether that department should hire Peter, Frank cannot felicitously utter 'Peter does not have good handwriting', on the grounds that to utter 'Peter has good handwriting' would implicate something false—namely, that Peter is not a good philosopher. So the fact that asserting *S* would implicate something false does not in general entitle us to assert its negation.

So Hawthorne's explanation does not rescue IRI from the putative counter-example raised by High Attributor–Low Subject Stakes. Hawthorne (2004: ch. 4, pp. 162–6) develops another line of argument that can be marshaled in support of IRI here, which he calls *projectivism*. The general projectivist strategy is to explain mistaken intuitions about knowledge by appeal to some psychological feature of speakers. Hawthorne's specific purpose is to provide a psychological explanation of 'our tendency to overproject our own lack of knowledge to others' (2004: 163). Applied to High Attributor–Low Subject Stakes, Hawthorne's explanation is that Hannah's increased awareness of the costs of being wrong leads her to overestimate the probability of counter-possibilities (2004: 164). So, Hannah overestimates the probability of the bank's changing its hours, and hence mistakenly concludes that Bill does not know that the bank will be open. Presumably the reason we find Hannah's judgment intuitively correct is that we follow Hannah in her overestimation of the probability of this counter-possibility.

One worry with this projectivist strategy has recently been raised by Keith DeRose (forthcoming). DeRose considers a case in which Hannah has much more evidence for her belief, and hence takes herself to know that the bank will be open, despite the high cost of being wrong. In such a circumstance, Hannah takes herself to know, but takes Bill (given his lesser evidence) not to know that the bank will be open. DeRose worries that the projectivist strategy cannot accommodate this type of data. Presumably, this is because Hannah is not projecting her *lack* of knowledge onto Bill, because, by assumption, Hannah knows that the bank will be open. Nevertheless, she falsely declares that Bill does not know that the bank will be open.

The version subject to DeRose's objection is, however, not the best version of the envisaged projectivist strategy. DeRose's point shows that Hawthorne is wrong to describe the problem as explaining the need to account for 'our tendency to overproject our own lack of knowledge to others'. For, as DeRose rightly points out, the phenomenon exists even when someone takes herself to know a certain proposition (because she satisfies the higher standards). The problem is rather to explain our tendency to overproject our evidentiary standards to other situations. And Hawthorne's explanation works equally well in this regard. Suppose that Hannah rightly takes herself to know that the bank will be open (because she has much more evidence than Bill). She might still deny knowledge to Bill, because she overestimates the probability that the bank has changed its hours. The consequence is that Hannah ends up projecting, not her *failure* to know, but the higher evidential standards required for her to know. That is, when we mistakenly overestimate the probability of counter-possibilities, we therefore mistakenly overproject higher evidentiary standards.

Thus, while DeRose's objection undermines the letter of Hawthorne's proposal, it does not undermine its spirit. Nevertheless, I am concerned about Hawthorne's proposal as a defense of IRI. If the explanation for our mistaken judgments in High Attributor–Low Subject Stakes is that we overestimate the probability of counter-possibilities, then it is hard to see why we should think that our judgments about High Stakes and Ignorant High Stakes are not similarly affected. That is, if conditions of risk make us overestimate counter-possibilities, why is it that Hannah does not after all know in High Stakes or Ignorant High Stakes? Perhaps in these cases too we are overestimating the probability of counter-possibilities, and Hannah does in fact know that the bank will be open (cf. MacFarlane 2005*a*; Williamson 2005). An adequate defense of IRI must proceed from assumptions that support the correctness of our intuitions in High Stakes and Ignorant High Stakes. My suspicion of the strategy is reinforced by the fact that, even when we have full knowledge of the likelihood of various counter-possibilities, it does not affect our judgments.

Here is an intuitively plausible account of what is occurring in High Attributor–Low Subject Stakes that is preferable to one that relies upon misjudging the likelihood of counter-possibilities.[8] Let us suppose that 'High Stakes' is a name for some person for whom the proposition *p* is a serious practical question. The account arises naturally from reflection upon the purposes someone in High Stakes' situation would have in enquiring whether

<hr />

[8] Thanks to Jeffrey King (p.c.) for helping me realize that this is the correct account of this case.

someone else knows that p. When High Stakes wants to know whether another person knows that p, it is presumably because High Stakes has an important decision to make, one that hinges upon whether or not p (this follows naturally from the fact that p is a serious practical question for High Stakes). So, High Stakes' interest lies in establishing p; that is, acquiring information that will allow her to know that p. What High Stakes is interested in finding out, then, is whether someone else's information state is sufficient for High Stakes to know that p. In short, the *purpose* High Stakes has in asking someone else whether or not p is true lies in finding out whether, *if that person had the interests and concerns High Stakes does*, that person would know that p. Since p is a serious practical question for High Stakes, she is not really worried about that person's own interests and concerns.

We now are in a possession of a perfectly intuitive explanation of the intuitions in High Attributor–Low Subject Stakes. Hannah and Sarah are worried about their impending bill, and so they want to know whether the bank will be open on Saturday. It is to resolve this question that they phone Bill. What they want to know from Bill is whether he has evidence such that, *were he in their practical situation*, it would suffice as knowledge. After all, they have to make a decision. Of course, were Bill to share Hannah and Sarah's practical situation, he *would* be in a High Stakes situation, and so would not know, on the basis of the evidence that he actually has, that the bank will be open on Saturday. So Hannah and Sarah are perfectly *correct* to conclude that the answer to their *actual* concern—whether Bill would know that the bank will be open if he were in Hannah and Sarah's practical situation—is negative.

This also explains our intuitions about the case, from a third-person perspective. When *we* are asked for our intuitions about the case, we intuitively recognize that what Hannah and Sarah *really* care about is whether Bill would know, were he in Hannah and Sarah's practical situation. We recognize that the answer to this is negative. That is, we recognize that the proposition that

Hannah and Sarah *really* want answered—*would Bill know were he in our practical situation*—is in fact false. So, we are strongly inclined to go along with Hannah and Sarah's judgments, since we recognize that they are perfectly correct about the information in which they are really interested.[9]

Unlike Hawthorne's proposed explanation for High Attributor–Low Subject Stakes, we do not need to appeal to an alleged psychological generalization that we always overestimate the likelihood of counter-possibilities (even when explicitly informed of their relative likelihood). There is also no threat of the sort envisaged in MacFarlane (2005a) and Williamson (2005) of this account generalizing to provide some alternative account of all of our shifting intuitions. In other words, the account explains clearly why we think Hannah and Sarah are in an important sense perfectly correct in denying knowledge to Bill, yet provides no comfort to someone who wishes to deny the accuracy of our intuitions about High Stakes, Ignorant High Stakes, and Low Attributor–High Subject Stakes. Indeed, it is crucial to my account that our intuitions in High Subject Stakes are correct, since that is what ultimately justifies our judgment that Hannah and Sarah are correct about what they care about—namely, whether Bill would know that the bank will be open, were he to share their interests and concerns.

Of course, the worry with solutions that do not overgeneralize is that they may undergeneralize. I have explained Hannah and Sarah's inclination to deny knowledge to Bill in High Attributor–Low Subject Stakes by appeal to the fact that, in that case, what is salient to them is a certain counterfactual question—namely, *if Bill shared their practical situation, would he know that the bank will be open?* But there are other cases in which people in High Stakes situations deny knowledge to others, where it may appear *ad hoc* to maintain that they want to use others as a source of informa-

---

[9] The same account smoothly explains Stewart Cohen's 'Airport Case', upon which High Attributor–Low Subject Stakes is based.

tion, as Hannah and Sarah use Bill in High Attributor–Low Subject Stakes. The worry then is that, in such cases, I must implausibly maintain that the interest of those in High Stakes situations is really in whether the subject of their knowledge attribution would know, were she in their practical situation.

However, even when those in High Stakes situations are not interested in using others as sources of information, their denials of knowledge to others are still interpretable as denials of the counterfactual I have discussed above. Perhaps the counterfactual is not salient to them, when they deny that someone knows. But that does not mean that the counterfactual does not guide their intuitions. Those in High Stakes situations are, by assumption, very concerned with the outcomes of their decisions. They are therefore unlikely to be merely concerned with whether others know, irrespective of how this fact may bear on their own situation. In a situation in which it is obvious that others lack new evidence, they might not seek to use these others as conduits of information, as Hannah and Sarah seek to use Bill in High Attributor–Low Subject Stakes. But the reason those in High Stakes situations deny that others know the answer to what is, for them, a serious practical question is still because the salient fact about the subject of the knowledge attribution is that she is not a useful conduit of information.

I have now developed one version of IRI, used it to explain the various intuitions discussed in the Introduction, and discussed some worries with it. I now turn to a thorough comparison between contextualist explanations of the examples we have been discussing and the explanations given by the advocate of IRI, with an eye towards evaluating the relative merits of the two positions.

6

Interest-Relative Invariantism versus Contextualism

My purpose in this chapter is to provide a thoroughgoing comparison between Interest-Relative Invariantism (IRI) and contextualism. My strategy will be to discuss putative costs and benefits of each doctrine, and argue that IRI has the overall advantage. There are several putative costs for IRI that contextualism does not appear to share. The first is that it yields some odd consequences for modal and temporal embeddings. The second is that it needs to be augmented with an alternative account of certain cases of the High Attributor–Low Subject Stakes variety. I will begin with a discussion of these two putative costs. I will argue that contextualism does not clearly fare better with modal and temporal embeddings. I then argue at some length that contextualism fares considerably worse on its explanation of the sort of intuitions with which we began. I then argue that there are costs to contextualism that are not shared by IRI. I conclude with a discussion of their respective treatments of epistemological skepticism.

The most obvious problem with IRI comes from the treatment of knowledge ascriptions in the scope of modal and temporal operators. According to IRI, for any p, $knowing$ that p is a property, possession of which at a time depends in part upon how much is at stake for that person at that time. This raises the following obvious modal objection to IRI. Suppose that Hannah knows at time t that the bank will be open on Saturday, on the basis of having been there on a Saturday two weeks earlier. Clearly, nothing much is then at stake for Hannah in the matter. The problem with IRI is that it countenances the truth of the following counterfactual:

(1) If Hannah had a bill coming due, then she wouldn't know that the bank would be open on Saturday.

According to IRI, whether a person N knows at a time t that p depends upon how much is at stake for N at time t. So, had more been at stake for Hannah at time t, merely having been to the bank on a previous Saturday would not be sufficient evidence for her to know that the bank would be open. So IRI entails the truth of (1).

IRI also seems to predict the truth of certain unintuitive past-tense claims. For example, suppose that on Thursday, Hannah had a bill coming due over the weekend. So, on Thursday, she did not know that the bank would be open on Saturday. But suppose that, on Friday, the company to whom the bill was owed decided to alleviate the debt of all of its customers. So, on Thursday, Hannah was in a High Stakes situation, whereas, on Friday, she was not. Then it would seem that IRI entails the truth of the following:

(2) Hannah didn't know on Thursday that the bank would be open on Saturday, but she did know on Friday.

That is, IRI seems to predict that (2) is true, even though Hannah had the same evidence on Friday as she did on Thursday, and nothing changed about the bank's opening hours. This is quite unintuitive.

The temporal case involves more complications than the modal case. Whether IRI entails the truth of (2) depends upon what one tak ˙ be the correct temporal metaphysics. For example, if one ᴜᴜnks that there are future facts, then it is a fact on Thursday that the company will alleviate the debt of all of its customers. If so, then perhaps Thursday is not a High Stakes situation for Hannah after all. Since whether IRI has unintuitive consequences in the temporal case depends upon debatable metaphysical issues, I will focus on IRI's unintuitive modal consequences in what follows.

On the face of it, contextualism does not appear to be burdened with the unintuitive consequences of IRI. Presumably, the reason it is not so burdened is similar to the reason that it is prima facie consistent with intellectualism. The interests of the person who asserts an instance of 'knows that p' determine the semantic value of her use of that expression. But the semantic value thereby determined is a property that is true of someone independently of what is at stake for that person. Whether a person N who truly believes that p has the property expressed by an occurrence of 'knows that p' depends only upon N's evidence for her true belief (though how much evidence she must have in order to have this property is of course determined by the nature of the property). Since in the envisaged counterfactual circumstance for (1), Hannah's evidence appears to be the same as it actually is, contextualism predicts that, if Hannah's interests were different, then the non-practical epistemological facts would remain the same. So contextualism does not entail the truth of (1).

Though plausible versions of contextualism do not entail the truth of (1), it is unclear whether contextualism is trouble free with regard to modal embeddings. If contextualism were true, it is not clear what the nature of the knowledge properties denoted by epistemic predicates would be. Since it is not evident what the nature of the knowledge properties denoted by epistemic predicates would be, predictions about the behavior of knowledge attributions under modal operators according to contextualism are excessively hasty.

On David Lewis's version of contextualism, the context-dependence of knowledge attributions is due to a tight analogy between knowledge attributions and quantifier phrases. On Lewis's view, 'S knows that p' is true relative to a context c if and only if p holds in every possibility in c left uneliminated by S's evidence; this is analogous with 'Every F is G' is true relative to a context c if and only if every F that is in the domain of c is G. So, to see how knowledge attributions should behave under modal operators, on a version of contextualism such as Lewis's, it would be useful to explore how sentences containing quantifier phrases behave under modal operators. This would provide some evidence about the nature of contextual restrictions of this kind.

Here is why it is useful for our purposes to explore how quantifier phrases behave when embedded under modal operators. Suppose that what we discover is that context provides as a quantifier domain a *property* that can take on different extensions relative to different circumstances of evaluation. In that case, Lewis's analogy to quantifier domains would suggest that what context provides in the case of knowledge ascriptions is a property as well, one that can take on different extensions relative to different circumstances of evaluation. If so, then there would be modal problems for Lewisian contextualism that are analogous to the modal problems facing IRI.

Given standard assumptions, a context-dependent expression receives its value from context before the sentence in which it is embedded is evaluated relative to other circumstances of evaluation. For example, consider the sentence 'I could have been a doctor'. This sentence, relative to a context of use in which Jason Stanley is the agent, expresses the proposition that it could have been the case that Jason Stanley is a doctor. To achieve this result, we are to think of context as first supplying a value to the context-dependent expression 'I'. The proposition that results from this assignment is then evaluated with respect to the modal operator. As a consequence of this, context-dependent expressions have the same semantic value relative to all circumstances of evaluation. We can use this fact to test whether the domain of a quantified noun phrase is a property or a set of objects.

Here is an example from Stanley and Szabo (2000: 252) that demonstrates that the domain of a quantified noun phrase is a property, rather than a set of contextually salient objects:

Suppose that John has a strange habit of buying exactly 70 bottles every time he goes to a supermarket. Suppose that John visits a supermarket that has exactly 70 bottles on the shelf, and purchases every bottle. Someone could then truly utter the sentence:

(37) If there were a few more bottles on the shelf, John would not have purchased every bottle.

However, if we assign to the contextual variable associated with 'every bottle' the set of bottles in the supermarket in the context of utterance of John's sentence, given the standard semantics for counterfactuals, (37) could not be truly uttered. To capture the reading of (37) on which it is true, one must treat the entity assigned to the contextual variable as a function from worlds and times to, say, the sets of bottles in the relevant supermarket at those worlds and times.

Stanley and Szabo's example, and others like it, demonstrate that what context provides as a domain for a quantified noun phrase is a property rather than a set of objects.

Given that context supplies properties as the domains of quantifiers, rather than sets of objects, if Lewis's analogy is apt, we should expect context to assign properties as epistemic domains as well, rather than sets of possibilities. I will first make a more general point, and then sharpen the point in light of the details of Lewis's theory. Suppose A is the agent of a particular context. The property that is the epistemic domain for an occurrence of an instance of 'knows that p' could, for example, be thought of as that expressed by 'is salient to A'. That is, 'S knows that p' is true relative to a context c if and only if p holds in every possibility salient to *A* left uneliminated by *S*'s evidence. Here, we are to think of 'salient to *A*' not as rigidly designating the set of possibilities actually salient to A, but rather as the property of *being salient to* A. Had things been different in certain ways, a different set of possibilities would be the possibilities salient to A (that is, the property would have had a different extension).

Suppose that it is a Friday, and Hannah is somewhat worried about a bill payment that she has sent off clearing her account. She is wondering whether to deposit her paycheck today, or wait until Saturday. Despite the fact that she has been to the bank before on a Saturday, it does not seem that she knows that the bank will be open on Saturday. But if the alleged context-sensitivity of knowledge ascriptions is modeled along the lines of quantifier domain restriction, then contextualism would entail the truth of the following:

(3) Hannah doesn't know that the bank will be open on Saturday. But if I wasn't aware that she had a bill coming due, she would know that the bank will be open on Saturday.

If the property that is the 'epistemic' domain for 'know that the bank will be open on Saturday' is the property of being a possibility salient to the speaker of (3), then, relative to a situation in which the speaker was not aware of the possibility that she has a bill coming due, this possibility would not be salient to the speaker. So, relative to such a situation, what is actually expressed by 'Hannah knows that the bank will be open on Saturday' would be true. This is a counter-intuitive consequence that parallels the counter-intuitive modal consequences that face the advocate of IRI.

Whether the contextualist faces such counter-intuitive consequences depends, of course, on her characterization of the nature of epistemic domains. But, if we think of epistemic domains on the model of quantifier domains, then the contextualist does face these consequences. We can make the point in detail by considering the particular contextualist theory provided by Lewis (1996). For Lewis, *S* knows at time *t* that *P* iff *S*'s evidence eliminates every possibility *that is not properly ignored at* t in which $\sim P$. The epistemic domain is therefore provided by the property of *not being properly ignored by the ascriber at the time of utterance*.[1] Lewis then provides a characterization of when a possibility is not properly ignored involving a series of seven rules. For our purposes, we may focus on the first rule he gives, the Rule of Actuality, which states that the possibility that actually obtains is never properly ignored. It is this rule that guarantees that knowledge is *factive*—namely, that knowing that *p* entails *p*. The Rule of Actuality guarantees that the extension of the property *not being properly ignored by the ascriber at the time of utterance* at the actual world contains the actual world.

Suppose that Hannah knows at time *t* that she is facing a computer screen. Then, her evidence will have eliminated every possibility in which she is not facing a computer screen that is in the actual extension of the property *not being properly ignored by the ascriber*. But, relative to other possible situations, the extension of this property is different. For example, if it had been the case that Hannah was in bed dreaming that she was facing a computer screen, having the same evidence, then she would not now know that she was facing a computer screen. But, if the extension of the property *not being properly ignored by the ascriber at the time of utterance* were the same in every possible world, then this counterfactual would be false, since Hannah's counterfactual evidence does eliminate every possibility in which she is not facing a computer screen that is in the actual extension of the property not *being properly ignored by the ascriber at the time of utterance*. In other words, if the extension of the property *not being properly ignored by the ascriber at the time of utterance* was the

---

[1] Where *t* is the time of utterance, and *N* the ascriber, the relevant property is more accurately described as *the property of not being properly ignored by* N *at* t. So the use of 'the ascriber' and 'the time of utterance' should be read as *de re* with respect to 'the property of'.

same with respect to every possible situation, then Hannah could know that *p* at a world *w*, even though *p* is false at *w*. This is an absurd consequence, and so Lewis's epistemic domains are, as one would expect from the analogy to quantifier domains, properties that have different extensions with respect to different possible worlds.

Perhaps a more straightforward way to make the point is as follows. The factivity of knowledge is not just a truth about knowledge, but a necessary truth about knowledge. That is, not only is it the case that *x*'s knowing that *p* entails that *p*, but it is necessarily true that if someone knows that *p*, then *p*. But if the epistemic domain of 'know' were the actual extension of the property *not properly ignored by the ascriber at the time of utterance*, then there would be counter-examples to the necessary factivity of knowledge. For there would be worlds at which someone knows that *p*, in virtue of having excluded the actual world of utterance, despite the fact that *p* is false relative to the counter-factual world.[2]

A similar point holds, *mutatis mutandis*, for Lewis's Rule of Belief, which states that a possibility that the subject believes to obtain is not properly ignored. If the extension of the property *not being properly ignored by the ascriber at the time of utterance* contained only the possibilities that the subject actually believed

---

[2] Anthony Gillies has pointed out to me that one could reply to this argument if one treated modal terms syntactically as quantifiers over situations or worlds. The thought behind this is that ordinary knowledge attributions contain a syntactically active parameter, which receives a set of epistemic possibilities as a value, relative to a context of use. But when knowledge attributions occur in modal contexts, the parameter is bound by the modal operator (so modals function as variable binders). This would secure the necessary factivity of knowledge, consistently with treating epistemic domains as sets rather than properties. But consider the following discourse:

A. If someone knows that *p*, then *p*.
B. What *A* said is necessarily true.

What *B* says is clearly true. But on Gillies's proposal, what *B* said is false.

to obtain, then someone could know that p, even though she did not believe that p.

When we look closely at Lewis's rules for determining the extension of the property *not being properly ignored by the ascriber at the time of utterance*, we see that they must be taken collectively to determine the extension of this property, relative to a circumstance of evaluation, on pain of allowing the disastrous consequence that someone could know that p despite the falsity of the proposition that p, or allowing that someone could know that p despite not believing that p. So we should take Lewis's Rule of Attention in a similar manner, as determining part of the extension of this property, relative to a context of use. Where S is the subject of the knowledge attribution, Lewis's Rule of Attention states that possibilities not being ignored by the ascriber are in the extension of the property *not being properly ignored by the ascriber at the time of utterance*. Lewis's rules uniformly determine the extension of this property, relative to a circumstance of evaluation. So, Lewis's theory has the consequence:

(4) Hannah doesn't know that p. But if we had been ignoring certain possibilities, then she would have known that p.

So Lewis's version of contextualism entails counterfactuals just as odd as those entailed by IRI.[3]

So much the worse for advocates of IRI and contextualism, one might suppose. However, this would be excessively hasty. As John Hawthorne (p.c.) has pointed out to me, many epistemological theories that are entirely independent of IRI or contextualism have equally worrisome modal consequences. For example, according to reliabilism, knowing that p requires that one's belief that p be the product of a reliable method. If one is

---

[3] Lewis could avoid this consequence, by treating the Rule of Attention differently from his other rules, e.g. by rigidifying on the possibilities salient to the conversational participants. But this involves the postulation of an ad-hoc asymmetry between the Rule of Attention and the other rules (thanks to Ted Sider for discussion here).

innocently traveling through Carl Ginet's fake barn country, where there are as many barn façades erected to trick the unwary as there are genuine barns, one's visual experience of a barn façade is not enough to know that one is seeing a barn, even when one is seeing a barn. Reliabilism captures this intuition, because, in Ginet's fake barn country, perception is not a reliable method. Nevertheless, we cannot say, of a person in fake barn country who is looking at a genuine barn:

(5) Poor Bill. He doesn't know that is a barn. But if there were fewer fake barns around then he would know that is a barn.

We do not take the fact that reliabilism entails the truth of (5) and similar apparently false counterfactuals to show that reliabilism is false. So it would be excessively hasty to take counterfactuals such as (1) as demonstrating the falsity of IRI.[4]

Let us now turn to a comparison between the account given by IRI of the intuitions we introduced in the Introduction and the account given by contextualism. As we have seen, the interest-relative invariantist must deny that our intuitions about cases such as High Attributor–Low Subject Stakes are to be taken at face value. The contextualist, in contrast, can accept these intuitions, and use them as evidence for her theory. If one's only concern is charity, this suggests an advantage for the contextualist.

As I have indicated several times, reasoning in this way mis-understands the role of these intuitions in the dialectic of the debate. My concern is not with bookkeeping, but rather with preserving the connection between knowledge and action. The intuitions with which we began are forceful, precisely because

---

[4] We can make these points with indicative conditionals such as 'If that is a barn, then if there are no fake barns around, then Bill knows it is a barn, but if there are fake barns around, then if that is a barn, Bill does not know it is a barn'. Such conditionals seem infelicitous, but they are perfectly true, if reliabilism is correct. Nevertheless, we do not take these facts to refute reliabilism.

they are exactly the intuitions we would expect to have if knowledge were connected with action. From the perspective that results from adopting the principle that one should act only on what one knows, the intuitions we have in High Attributor–Low Subject Stakes look to be clearly mistaken. That is, from this perspective, we should seek an account that does not yield a charitable account of this class of intuitions.

Be that as it may, there are cases exactly parallel to High Attributor–Low Subject Stakes in which the contextualist can provide no easy explanation of our intuitions. Consider the following scenario:

*High Attributor–Low Subject Stakes**

It is Friday, and Bill is considering going to the bank. Nothing much hangs on whether he gets to the bank before Monday. So he considers delaying going to the bank until Saturday. He has been to the bank before on Saturday, and found it open. So he assumes it will be open the next day (and it will). He utters absent-mindedly, 'Well, since I know the bank will be open tomorrow, I'll just go tomorrow.' In contrast, it is very important for Hannah to get to the bank before Monday. She overhears Bill, and asks him what the basis for his claim was. But she too has been to the bank on previous Saturdays, which does not allay her concern that the bank has changed its hours. She therefore concludes that what Bill said was false.

Intuitively, Hannah is right to conclude that Bill's utterance was false. But contextualism predicts that she is wrong. Since nothing is at stake for Bill if he does not make it to the bank until Monday, he is in a 'low standards' context, and he does have sufficient justification to stand in the relation expressed by 'know', relative to that context, to the proposition that the bank will be open. So what Bill said was true. Contextualism must explain our tendency to make errors in this kind of case, even given full knowledge of all of the facts. In High Attributor–Low Subject Stakes*, the contextualist will appeal to semantic blindness, and the advocate of IRI will appeal to the explanation given in the preceding section.

Indeed, just as IRI delivers an apparently incorrect verdict on High Attributor–Low Subject Stakes, contextualism yields an apparently incorrect verdict on High Attributor–Low Subject Stakes*. So in every kind of case that poses a prima facie problem for IRI, there is a translation scheme to a precisely parallel case that poses the same sort of problem for contextualism. But there are several kinds of cases (for example, cases like Low Subject–High Attributor Stakes and Ignorant High Stakes) that pose problems for contextualism, but that are smoothly handled (without an appeal to an error theoretic explanation) by IRI. The existence of this translation scheme poses a significant problem for the contextualist who seeks to gain an advantage over the advocate of IRI by appeal to her more charitable account of High Attributor–Low Subject Stakes.

Moreover, the contextualist explanation in terms of general semantic blindness is considerably more disruptive to our conceptual scheme than the explanation suggested by IRI. Semantic blindness involves the dramatic claim that we are blind to the semantic workings of our language, and we make errors about the truth value of knowledge ascriptions as a result of that blindness. In contrast, the explanation I have provided of High Attributor–Low Subject Stakes is not similarly disruptive; I have not attributed to people a new kind of hitherto unforeseen error. People ignore some of the metaphysical determinants of knowledge, rather than being ignorant of features of their language. The reason we have the intuitions we do about High Attributor–Low Subject Stakes is that Hannah and Sarah are correct about what they care about—namely, whether or not Bill would know that the bank will be open, were he in their practical situation. We recognize that they are completely correct about this, so we do not balk at their false claim. This is certainly an error theory, but it does not involve imputation to agents of a hitherto unknown form of linguistic ignorance.

The next point is that, if the contextualist abandons the intention-based thesis about context-sensitive expressions in order to capture Ignorant High Stakes, then there is a parallel strategy available to the advocate of IRI to capture High Attributor–Low Subject Stakes. As we have seen in Chapter 1, given plausible assumptions about what fixes the semantic content of context-sensitive expressions, relative to a context, contextualism yields incorrect results about examples such as Ignorant High Stakes. That is, if, as many theorists believe, the intention-based view of context-sensitive expressions is correct, contextualism delivers incorrect results about this case. Since Hannah and Sarah are unaware of the costs of being wrong, their mental states (on the intention-based view of context-sensitive expressions) determine the 'low-stakes' semantic value for 'know the bank will be open'. Hence the contextualist predicts his or her utterance expresses a truth. But intuitively what Hannah says is false.

In contrast, the version of IRI that I have presented delivers a perfectly correct account of our intuitions about Ignorant High Stakes. Since Hannah and Sarah, unbeknownst to them, are in a high-stakes situation, they must have more evidence in order to know that the bank will be open. Thus, IRI captures our intuitions about this case without having to reject any independently motivated semantic theses, such as the intention-based view of context-sensitive expressions.

But, if we abstract from the cost of rejecting the intention-based view of context-sensitive expressions, IRI still fares well against a version of contextualism that abandons the intention-based view of context-sensitive expressions. On this version of contextualism, it is the *actual* interests of the participants in the conversational context that determine the semantic value of 'know', relative to a context, rather than what the participants perceive their interests to be. Since it is in Hannah's interests (whether she knows it or not) to make it to the bank as soon as possible, she counts as being in a 'high-stakes' context, despite her ignorance of this fact. The very fact that she is in a high-stakes context makes it the case that the semantic value of her use of 'know' is a relation that requires higher evidentiary standards than usual. So, on this version of contextualism, Hannah's assertion is false, as intuition suggests. This view is tantamount to a rejection of the intention-based view of context-sensitive expressions, because the semantic content of 'know' can be determined by factors independent of the mental states of any users in the context, as in this envisaged analysis of Ignorant High Stakes.

If the contextualist is allowed this sort of maneuver, then the advocate of IRI can make similar claims about what features of a subject's situation have the function of raising evidentiary standards. If such maneuvers are legitimate, the interest-relative invariantist can provide a straightforward account of High Attributor–Low Subject Stakes.

The reason that the interest-relative invariantist cannot provide a straightforward account of High Attributor–Low Subject Stakes, one that does not appeal to mistaken beliefs, is that, intuitively speaking, it does not matter to Bill whether or not the bank will be open on Saturday. So he needs only to meet ordinary standards in order to know that the bank will be open. But this result depends upon what we take Bill's interests and concerns to be. If we include Hannah and Sarah's interests *among* Bill's interests and concerns, then it will follow that it does matter to him whether or not the bank is open. On the strength-of-evidence version of IRI sketched above, this would take the form of making it such that Hannah and Sarah's situation affects the warranted expected utilities of the actions at Bill's disposal. If we include among Bill's interests what will happen to Hannah and Sarah, and we expand the scope of the 'actions at Bill's disposal' to include the action of acquiring more information about whether the bank is open and then informing Hannah and Sarah, the interest-relative invariantist can capture High Attributor–Low Subject Stakes.[5]

---

[5] Of course, as I have been suggesting throughout, we should not seek a charitable account of these intuitions.

By expanding the scope of what counts as a subject's interests at a time, we can make IRI flexible enough to give a straightforward account of High Attributor–Low Subject Stakes. Of course, such an expansion of Bill's interests (or the actions at his disposal) is unintuitive. Indeed, it is just as unintuitive as a contextualist's rejection of the intention-based view of context-sensitive terms in order to accommodate Ignorant High Stakes. Just as contextualism allows for flexibility in selecting which features of the utterance context are relevant for determining the semantic value of instances of 'knows that p', IRI allows for flexibility in selecting which features of a putative knower's situation determine how good her evidence must be in order to know. Such features could, in principle, be highly relational properties of her situation. Since defenders of either view can exploit the relevant flexibility for (perhaps illegitimate) theoretical gain, the contextualist gains no advantage on this score.

In sum, the interest-relative invariantist's account of the ordinary cases we have discussed concerning knowledge attributions seems clearly superior to the contextualist's. The one kind of case that is prima facie problematic for the interest-relative invariantist is High Attributor–Low Subject Stakes. Since this is the one case that is *not* attributable to our commitment to the principle that one should act only upon what one knows, it does not count in favor of a theory that it gives a charitable account of it. The source of our intuitions about High Attributor–Low Subject Stakes is distinct from the source of our intuitions about the other cases. One should therefore expect a distinct account of the source of our intuitions in this case, and that is what IRI entails.

Furthermore, for every High Attributor–Low Subject Stakes sort of case, there is a *precisely analogous case* (e.g. High Attributor–Low Subject Stakes*) where the contextualist produces a similar verdict to IRI. So it is hardly to the contextualist's advantage to advertise her charitable account of cases of this form. In addition, the fact that the contextualist provides an asymmetrical treatment of High Attributor–Low Subject Stakes and High

Attributor–Low Subject Stakes[*] strongly suggests that there is something wrong with the explanation, even when it is more 'charitable'. There are also a number of types of cases (for example, of the form of Low Attributor–High Subject Stakes and Ignorant High Stakes) that IRI smoothly handles, and contextualism does not. Finally, the explanation for High Attributor–Low Subject Stakes available to the advocate of IRI possesses independent plausibility that is not shared by the considerably more radical thesis of semantic blindness.

The interest-relative invariantist also possesses an advantage over the contextualist for other reasons. The contextualist's claim that knowledge attributions are context-sensitive in a distinctively epistemological way (perhaps because 'know' is itself a context-sensitive word) leaves her with a semantic burden. The contextualist discharges this burden principally by appeal to her account of ordinary cases such as the ones with which we began this book. But, since IRI can give a superior account of these cases, the contextualist is robbed of her evidence for contextualism.

In contrast with contextualism, the advocate of IRI has no semantic burden to discharge. IRI is not a semantic thesis at all; it is rather a metaphysical thesis about the nature of the knowledge relation. The claim that whether someone knows at time t that p depends upon facts about that person is, of course, uncontroversial. IRI states only that there are certain traditionally non-epistemic properties of a person's situation that help determine whether or not that person knows the proposition in question. So, while IRI entails the controversial epistemological thesis that knowledge is sensitive to the costs of being wrong, it is a semantically innocent thesis.

Here is an analogy that helps shed light upon the respective semantic commitments of IRI and contextualism.[6] Suppose

---

[6] I arrived at this analogy by reflection upon Brian Weatherson's analogy, discussed on his blog http://tar.weatherson.net, between contextualism and a 'fixed-speed' account of running. I think the analogy I have chosen is better for certain reasons I will not discuss here

someone suggested that whether x hits y is determined by a situation-invariant level of force with which x makes contact with y:

Fixed Force. Hits $<x, y, t, w>$ if and only if x makes contact with y at t and w with a force greater than N.

The fixed-force account of hitting is implausible. Whether x hits y depends not just on the force with which x makes contact with y, but on other features of x's situation—for example, x's intentions in making contact with y. If someone pushes me into Fred, I have not hit Fred, even though, had I intentionally made contact with Fred in the same manner, I would have hit Fred.

The fixed-force account of hitting is roughly analogous to an account of knowledge according to which whether a true belief constitutes knowledge is just a matter of truth-conducive factors, either objectively or from the point of view of the subject (I say 'roughly', because of course intellectualism is prima facie much more plausible than the fixed-force account of hitting). According to each theory, having the property is just a matter of some factor X, and the opponent of the theory wishes to establish that there is an additional relevant factor Y. We can call the opponent of the fixed-force account of hitting an 'interest-relative invariantist' about hitting, but that would be giving a grandiose name to a non-grandiose position. IRI about knowledge should also not be thought of as a grandiose *semantic* claim, a distinctive new semantic analysis of the verb 'know'. It is rather just the metaphysical claim that there are non-truth-conducive factors at play in determining whether someone knows a true proposition he or she believes.[7]

---

[7] Neta (forthcoming) argues that 'sees' is a context-sensitive verb, via construction of a skeptical argument that can be blocked by appeal to context-sensitivity. I do not find Neta's argument particularly persuasive, since I am not moved by his 'No Difference Principle'. But in any case it seems to me that the most persuasive examples in his paper can be treated by recognizing that seeing is an interest-relative relation.

These points also show why it is misleading to call IRI 'Subject-Sensitive Invariantism', as many theorists do. Of course, according to IRI, whether x knows that p will depend upon facts about x. So, IRI is a theory according to which whether x knows that p is dependent upon facts about the subject of the putative knowing. But every coherent theory of knowledge is such that whether someone knows that p will depend upon facts about that person. It is certainly not the sensitivity to facts about the subject of the putative knowing that makes IRI distinctive. It is rather sensitivity to certain *non-traditional* facts about the subject—namely, the subject's practical interests.

Just as there is no special semantic burden of proof on someone who rejects the fixed-force account of hitting, so there is no special semantic burden of proof on someone who rejects the fixed-evidence account of knowledge in favor of IRI. Rejecting these accounts does not entail a commitment to placing the relevant expression into some special linguistic category. IRI is not a semantic claim at all. It is just a claim about what kinds of facts about the subject and her environment make it the case that she knows. In contrast, contextualism is a special semantic claim, for which the contextualist is committed to providing linguistic evidence. And, as we have seen, the linguistic evidence in support of it is weak.

The fact that contextualism is a special semantic claim leads me to the next point, which is that contextualism, unlike IRI, is an instance of a general method of resolving any conflicting claims. Suppose we have two claims, S and not-S. It is always open to someone to resolve the apparent conflict by maintaining that the two occurrences of 'S' in the claims express different propositions, relative to their differing contexts of use. It is for this reason that there are contextualist accounts of every extant philosophical problem, from ethical disputes to the sorites and the liar paradoxes. This places a special burden on any particular contextualist resolution of apparently conflicting claims. The special burden is to show that one is not appealing to the all-purpose method of evading apparent conflict.

IRI does not face this concern, as IRI is not an instance of a strategy generally available for evading all apparent conflicts. As we will see in the final chapter, IRI is not an option available in the case of, for example, the sorites paradox. And, as I have indicated in a previous chapter, there is no coherent interest-relative-invariantist account of the liar paradox. IRI is an available option in the case of knowledge only because of special features of the case. Since IRI is not a special semantic thesis that is an application of a general strategy for avoiding apparent conflict, there is no additional burden on its advocates.

The case for the superiority of IRI over contextualism therefore does not depend upon its superior treatment of certain problem cases, such as Ignorant High Stakes and Low Attributor–High Subject Stakes. Even if one did not share the intuitions about these cases, or had theoretical reasons for dispensing with them, there is still a powerful case to be made for IRI over contextualism.[8] Even if no weight at all is given to the intuitions about Ignorant High Stakes and Low Attributor–High Subject Stakes, the case for IRI is not substantially weakened.

IRI is not a special semantic thesis. But it does entail the falsity of a prima facie plausible epistemic thesis—namely the intellectualist thesis that whether a true belief constitutes knowledge is

[8] For example, DeRose (forthcoming: sect. 2) argues that we should give less weight to intuitions about the *falsity* of claims than we do to intuitions about the *truth* of claims. Ignorant High Stakes and Low Attributor-High Subject Stakes are the only two cases in which speakers assert something, and we intuitively think the things they say are false. In the other cases, speakers assert something, and we intuitively think the things they say are true. Given DeRose's methodological scruples, then, we should give these intuitions less weight. I should add that I am suspicious of DeRose's methodological claim here, since it makes an uncomfortable distinction between intuitions we have that assertions of negated propositions are true (which are, according to him, trustworthy) and intuitions that assertions of non-negated propositions are false (which are, according to him, untrustworthy).

not affected by practical facts. This is a cost. But the nature of the cost depends upon whether the advocate of IRI also thinks that other epistemic notions are similarly interest-relative. In neither case is the denial of intellectualism too costly.

Suppose that one is attracted to intellectualism about some central epistemic notions, such as evidence. One can still consistently accept IRI about knowledge. For IRI about knowledge is only the thesis that intellectualism is false about *knowledge*. For example, on the version of IRI developed in the previous chapter, a person's interests determine only how much evidence he or she must have in order to know a true proposition he or she believes. Once the interests have determined the evidential status one must have in order to know, they quietly march out of the door, leaving the 'pure' epistemic notion of evidence to do the rest of the work. Insofar as one is attracted to the preservation of the intellectualist thesis for some epistemic notion, it is possible to preserve intellectualism about evidence and justification, consistently with IRI about knowledge.

On the other hand, suppose (as I think overwhelmingly plausible) that all normal epistemic notions are interest-relative. In this case, it is no longer clear what the intuitive claim is that the advocate of IRI supposedly denies. It is not the claim that (Gettier cases aside) one person can know that *p* while another person with the same evidence for her true belief that *p* does not know that *p*. If all epistemic notions are interest-relative, then evidence is interest-relative as well. If evidence shares the interest-relativity of knowledge, then two people who do not share the same practical situation will not in general have the same evidence. So, whether one advocates a more restricted form of IRI just about knowledge, or the broader form I favor that encompasses all epistemic notions, the denial of intellectualism is not an unacceptable cost.

However, of course I do not mean to claim that, from the perspective of the intellectual, IRI is not a more radical epistemological thesis than contextualism. To see that IRI makes a considerably more extreme epistemological claim than the context-ualist makes, consider the following analogy. Suppose, pointing at a wooden table, I utter 'that table is made of wood'. It is uncontroversial that the truth of my *utterance* does depend upon interests, since my interests and intentions determine the seman-tic value of the demonstrative expression 'that table'. But the truth of the proposition expressed, that that table is made of wood, does *not* depend upon interests; denying this would be an extreme metaphysical claim. Similarly, from the perspective of intellectualism about knowledge, standard contextualism is *not* an extreme metaphysical claim, since it is analogous with the metaphysically innocuous point that the truth of utterances of 'that table is made of wood' is dependent upon interests, while the truth of the proposition expressed is not.[9] However, from the perspective of intellectualism about knowledge, IRI *is* an extreme metaphysical claim, analogous to the claim that the truth of the proposition expressed by an utterance of 'that table is made of wood' is dependent upon interests.

The preservation of intellectualism about knowledge is not the only putative attraction of contextualism with no interest-relative analogue. For the contextualist offers a diagnosis of the skeptical problematic. If there is no interest-relative alterna-tive to the contextualist's diagnosis, that might favor the context-ualist position.

There is some initial promise to an interest-relative explan-ation of the grip of skepticism. It is very intuitive to suppose that, where ordinary action is concerned, skeptical scenarios are not serious practical questions. Furthermore, the fact that skepticism is most worrying to those whose job it is to address it—namely, working epistemologists—may seem to show some difference between the circumstances in which it is a serious practical question, and the circumstances in which it is not.

[9] I say 'standard contextualism' because it is, of course, consistent with contextualism that the denoted knowledge relations are themselves interest-relative.

If one wished to generate the contextualist-like result that epistemologists' knowledge claims are generally false, without impugning ordinary knowledge claims, one might try to pursue the following path. When an epistemologist who takes skepticism seriously is thinking about skepticism at a given time, her practical goals and interests are directed towards resolving skepticism, via arguments that would convince a skeptic. Given such practical goals and interests, the proposition that she is a brain in a vat may be a serious practical alternative to her belief that she has hands. Furthermore, given her goals and interests, she presumably must have a great deal of evidence against this alternative, perhaps non-question-begging evidence that deductively entails that she is not a brain in a vat.

This is an attractive approach. But it is also seriously incomplete. One would need to explicate the notion of a serious practical question so that skeptical propositions are not serious practical questions for non-epistemologists, while they are for epistemologists when they are reflecting upon skepticism. This is no simple task. First, it is not clear that the notion of a serious practical question can be spelled out in such a way as ever to exclude all skeptical propositions. Secondly, if it can, it is not clear that the resulting notion of a serious practical question will help us justify the claim that skeptical propositions are serious practical questions for the epistemologist.

An advocate of IRI who seeks to preserve the truth of ordinary knowledge claims must explain why, in an ordinary case, a skeptical scenario is not a serious practical alternative to one's ordinary beliefs. And this is, of course, difficult. Consider, for example, the account of serious practical questions I gave above, in terms of warranted expected utility. The possibility that I am a brain in a vat would not be irrelevant for the warranted expected utilities of the actions at my disposal. Many of my actions—for example, my altruistic ones—have far less utility relative to a state of the world in which I am a brain in a vat. Only an implausibly narrow conception of utility, of the sort we associate with hedonistic act utilitarianism, could preclude this result. Furthermore, there are skeptical scenarios that clearly would have drastic effects on the utility of my actions, even as conceived of 'from the inside'. For example, consider the skeptical possibility that I am a brain in a vat about to be horrifically tortured if I do not make as if to raise my right arm now. This scenario would affect the utilities of the actions at my disposal, even as conceived of 'from the inside'.

One promising avenue for treating this problem for an interest-relative-invariantist reply to skepticism is suggested by reflection upon the asteroid case discussed in the previous chapter. I am not rationally obliged to take into account in my present actions the possibility of an asteroid strike on New York City within the next twenty-four hours. Presumably, the reason is that, relative to the evidence scientists possess, the likelihood of such an event occurring is very small. Suppose it could be argued that, relative to the evidence we ought to possess, the probability of a skeptical scenario occurring is sufficiently small (given perhaps some sufficiently objective sense of probability). If so, then skeptical scenarios will not have an effect on the warranted expected utilities of the actions at my disposal. Then, despite the fact that the obtaining of a skeptical proposition might adversely affect the utility of some of the actions at my disposal, their extremely low probability would exclude them from being serious practical questions. In short, skeptical propositions would not be propositions that I am rationally obligated to consider in my current decision making, for the same reason that I am not rationally obliged to consider in my current decision making the possibility that an asteroid will wipe out New York City in the next twenty-four hours (whatever explains *that*).

However, this is only a response to the less interesting skeptic. The less interesting skeptic grants that we do have good evidence against the obtaining of skeptical propositions. But she argues that we still do not have enough evidence to *know* that skeptical propositions do not obtain. What I have sketched is not a response to the most pernicious skeptic, who holds that we have *no evidence at all* against the obtaining of skeptical propositions. There is nothing in the version of IRI that I sketched in Chapter 5 that helps against this version of skepticism. The advocate of this sort of 'strength-of-evidence' IRI must adopt some other strategy against those who maintain that we have no evidence at all against the obtaining of skeptical scenarios.[10]

So the 'strength-of-evidence' version of IRI that I sketched in Chapter 5 can at best be used to respond to the less interesting version of skepticism, according to which we do have evidence against the obtaining of skeptical scenarios, but not enough evidence to know that they do not obtain. But 'strength-of-evidence' versions of contextualism that appeal to higher-and lower-standard knowledge relations also are only designed as responses to this version of skepticism. According to the more interesting skeptic, our ordinary perceptual evidence provides us with *no good reason* at all to believe (for example) that we have hands (cf. Klein 2000: 110). On this view, it is not because I lack enough evidence that I do not know that I have hands. Rather, perception provides me with no evidence at all that I have hands. But contextualists who hold that the different knowledge relations are graded according to epistemic strength do not have a response to this version of skepticism. So contextualists of this variety have had to provide different responses to it. For example, Stewart Cohen argues that it is a priori rational to believe that

---

[10] It is furthermore not clear that, on the resulting notion of serious practical question, we can say that skeptical propositions are serious practical questions for epistemologists currently thinking about skepticism. After all, the probability of these propositions remains equally low for these epistemologists, relative to the evidence they ought to possess. It does not follow from the fact that epistemologists currently thinking about skepticism care more about it that the truth or falsity of these propositions will affect the utility of the actions at their disposal more than the utility of ordinary citizens (though *establishing* the truth or falsity of skeptical propositions might). Perhaps there is some elaborate story to be told here in defense of this position, but I won't bother exploring it here.

I have some evidence that I am not a brain in a sophisticated vat (e.g. Cohen 1999: 68 ff.). But Cohen certainly does not use the contextualist machinery to justify this claim; whatever its other merits, this response to skepticism is entirely independent of Cohen's contextualism. So strength-of-evidence contextualism fares no better in responding to skepticism than strength-of-evidence IRI.[11]

The fact that strength-of-evidence versions of contextualism face the same problems addressing skepticism as strength-of-evidence versions of IRI raises the suspicion that it is not the contextualist aspect of contextualist proposals that does the work in addressing skepticism, but rather features that are common between contextualism and IRI. If so, then the advocate of IRI can mimic contextualist responses to skepticism, if she desires.

---

[11] According to Neta (2003), the effect of considering skeptical scenarios is to change what counts as evidence, so that it is no longer permissible to take ordinary perceptual experience as evidence for (e.g.) my belief that I have hands. First, Neta argues that for S to have evidence for p is for S to have evidence that favors p over some alternatives that are relevant in the context of epistemic appraisal. Then, he argues that, by considering skeptical scenarios, the skeptic forces us to work with a concept of evidence according to which my normal perceptual experiences do not count as evidence at all for (e.g.) my perceptual belief that I have hands. So, Neta's version of contextualism promises to account for the strongest version of skepticism, according to which our ordinary perceptual experience does not count as evidence at all for the belief that there is an external world. But, whatever its success as a diagnosis of skepticism, Neta's version of contextualism is not acceptable as an account of the ordinary cases that motivate it. Consider, (e.g.) our intuition in High Stakes that Hannah does not know that the bank will be open, since the cost of being wrong is high. Relative to this situation, the relevant alternative is that (e.g.) the bank has changed its hours. Neta's view entails that our reaction to this situation should be to say that Hannah has *no evidence at all* that the bank will be open on Saturday (since Hannah's previous visit to the bank on a Saturday is not evidence for the hypothesis that the bank will be open on Saturday rather than the hypothesis that the bank changed its hours). But that is simply not our reaction to this case. We believe that Hannah has perfectly good evidence for her belief that the bank will be open, but it is not *enough* evidence for her to know that the bank will be open.

For example, the version of contextualism presented in Lewis (1996) does account for the more interesting version of skepticism discussed above. But here it seems clear that the interest-relative invariantist can co-opt Lewis's resources to deliver a similar response.

According to Lewis's *Rule of Attention*, any possibility that is not being ignored is not properly ignored. It is the rule of attention that does the bulk of the work in Lewis's response to skepticism. When epistemologists are discussing skeptical possibilities, they cannot properly ignore them, since they are not in fact ignoring them. Since Lewis is a contextualist, he interprets proper ignoring in contextualist terms; it is a matter of the possibilities properly ignored by the knowledge attributor. But insofar as the interest-relative invariantist is attracted to Lewis's response to skepticism, she can appropriate the resources he has developed. For example, she can construe Lewis's notion of *proper ignoring* in terms of what the subject of the knowledge attribution may properly ignore, rather than the attributor. She can also adopt a suitably modified version of the rule of attention: what the subject is not in fact ignoring is not properly ignored by the subject (cf. Hawthorne 2004: 158–9), on the 'subject-sensitive salience constraint'). It will then turn out that, when an epistemologist is discussing skepticism, her attributions of knowledge to anyone listening to her will turn out to be false, since her audience will not be ignoring skeptical possibilities (and hence such possibilities will not be properly ignored, by the interest-relative version of the rule of attention).

The problems facing certain IRI accounts of skepticism are equally problems for similar versions of contextualism. Furthermore, the resources contextualists have used to address skepticism can be mimicked by the interest-relative invariantist. Therefore, no advantage of contextualism over IRI is to be found by consideration of the contextualist's treatment of skepticism.

7

Interest-Relative Invariantism versus Relativism

Any version of Interest-Relative Invariantism (IRI) will have certain unintuitive consequences. I have tried to argue that it is not clear that the unintuitive consequences of IRI are any worse than the unintuitive consequences of other standard epistemological theories. But one might think that these shortcomings with IRI, together with the worries we have raised for contextualism and strict invariantism, motivate a different approach altogether. Perhaps the contextualist and interest-relative invariantist are right, as against the strict invariantist, that the truth of knowledge attributions does shift in the ways suggested by our stock of examples. But perhaps there is a way of adding on an additional parameter of variation that allows us to evade the unintuitive consequences of IRI. This is precisely the reaction of John MacFarlane (2005a), who has, together with Mark Richard (2004), advanced the doctrine of *relativism about knowledge attributions* as a new alternative.

Rather than adopt MacFarlane's or Richard's formulations and risk the possibility of misinterpretation, I will describe the doctrine(s) as I would formulate them. To describe and evaluate the various possible implementations of relativism properly, I will need first to introduce some theoretical and historical context.[1]

We have been assuming in this book a theory of content that is descended in large part from the informal remarks in Kaplan (1989). According to this theory, a sentence expresses a proposition relative to a context of use (and may express distinct propositions relative to distinct contexts, as with context-sensitive sentences such as 'I am tired'). A proposition is the ultimate bearer of truth value and what is said by a sentence, relative to a context of use. Relative to different circumstances of evaluation, a proposition may take on different truth values. For example, relative to a world in which I became a cellist instead of a philosopher, the proposition now expressed by my utterance of 'I am a philosopher' would be false.

In Kaplan's original work, he took the features of circumstances of evaluation to be times and places, in addition to worlds. For this reason, his 'propositions' were rather gerrymandered entities. For example, the proposition expressed by 'It is raining', for Kaplan, was a function from location, time, and world triples

---

[1] MacFarlane uses terminology differently from the way I do, and would reject my characterizations of relativism. But I reject his reasons for so doing. MacFarlane thinks that my characterization of relativism does not distinguish between what he calls relativism, and what he calls 'use-sensitivity' (MacFarlane 2005b). But I see no interest to his notion of use-sensitivity, nor cause for seeing this artificial notion as a species of context-sensitivity (e.g. on his use of the term 'context-sensitivity', *virtually every traditionally eternal sentence counts as context-sensitive*). In defense of his broad use of 'context-sensitivity', MacFarlane has pointed out (p.c.) that Lewis regards contingency as a species of indexicality. But this is due to modal realism. For Lewis, if quantifiers are read unrestrictedly, sentences have their truth-values necessarily. So, according to modal realism, contingency does result from a kind of context-sensitivity—namely, quantifier domain restriction. Non-modal realists cannot appeal to Lewis's claim as a defense of an implausibly broad usage of 'context-sensitivity'. Nevertheless, despite my different use of terminology, the objections I make below apply to his positive view.

to truth values (Kaplan (1989: 504). But, as Kaplan himself recognized, his use of the term 'proposition' was not the 'classical use' (ibid.). According to the classical use of 'proposition', a proposition is not true or false relative to a time or a place, but true 'without qualification'. As Frege (1979: 135) so clearly puts the point:

It is of the essence of a thought to be non-temporal and non-spatial. In the case of the thought that $3 + 4 = 7$ and the laws of nature there is hardly any need to support this statement. If it should turn out that the law of gravitation ceased to be true from a certain moment onwards, we should conclude that it was not true at all, and put ourselves out to discover a new law: the new one would differ in containing a condition which would be satisfied at one time but not at another. It is the same with place. If it should transpire that the law of gravitation was not valid in the neighborhood of Sirius, we should search for another law which contained a condition that was satisfied in our solar system but not in the neighborhood of Sirius. If someone wished to cite, say, 'The total number of inhabitants of the German Empire is 52000000' as a counterexample to the timelessness of thoughts, I should reply: This sentence is not a complete expression of a thought at all, since it lacks a time-determination. If we add such a determination, for example 'at noon on 1 January 1897 by central European time', then the thought is either true, in which case it is always, or better, timelessly true, or it is false and in that case it is false without qualification.

Much work in the years following the distribution of Kaplan (1989) was devoted to replacing Kaplan's non-eternal propositions with more eternal entities that embody our intuitions that what is said and what is believed are true *simpliciter*, rather than relative to times or places. Authors such as Mark Richard (1981, 1982) and Nathan Salmon (1986) provided semantic theories that distinguished between genuine propositions, on the one hand, whose truth was only relative to possible worlds, and more gerrymandered entities, such as functions from times and locations to genuine propositions, on the other.

An assumption David Kaplan and Mark Richard make is that tenses and location expressions such as 'somewhere' and 'in Scotland' are *sentence operators*.[2] By 'sentence operator', I will mean an expression that takes as its value some semantic value of the sentence it embeds, relative to a context of use, and yields a semantic value as an output. So, for example, the modal operator 'It is necessary that' can be thought of as expressing a function from semantic values to semantic values, whose output is true relative to a world if and only if its input is true relative to every possible world, and is otherwise false relative to that world. Similarly, we can think of the past tense as the sentence operator 'It was the case that', which expresses a function from semantic contents of sentences relative to a context to semantic values. The output of this function is true relative to a time t if and only if the input semantic content, as applied to some time prior to t, either yields true as a value, or yields a true proposition as a value.

Kaplan took both modals and tenses to be sentence operators, and furthermore took them both as operating on the same entity, his *sentence contents*. He also treated locational expressions such as 'somewhere' and 'Two miles north it is the case that' in this manner. On this model, it is most helpful to think of sentence contents as functions from the kinds of things operators implicitly involve (for example, worlds, times, locations) to truth values. So on a natural way of thinking of Kaplan's semantics, sentence contents are functions from worlds, times, locations, and perhaps other elements (cf. Lewis 1981) to truth values.[3]

---

[2] Nathan Salmon (1989: 386 n. 31) rejects the thesis that ordinary English tenses are sentential operators, and takes them to be operators on predicates instead (in his fragment in the appendix to Salmon (1986), he does not actually include basic tenses). So Salmon does not share the assumption that tenses are sentential operators. But he still treats them as operators, rather than variable binders or predicates, and so this difference is inessential to the discussion that follows.

[3] I am ignoring for illustrative purposes the fact that in his informal remarks Kaplan expresses the desire for his contents to be structured. This feature of

Richard and Salmon also take modals and tenses to be operators. But, since they want to preserve a place for the classical unrelativized notion of content, they multiply the kinds of semantic contents sentences have, relative to a context of use. For both Richard and Salmon, a sentence not only expresses a classical proposition, relative to a context of use, but also expresses a *temporal semantic value*. We can think of these temporal semantic values as functions from times (and perhaps locations) to classical propositions (the truth of which is not relative to anything but possible worlds). If we treat tenses such as 'It was the case that' and 'It will be the case that' and locational operators such as 'somewhere' as sentence operators, as Richard does, then such operators do not operate on genuine propositions, but rather on temporal semantic values (similarly, tenses for Salmon would operate on time-functional predicate-level semantic values).

So, on Kaplan's view, the truth of a proposition is relative to a time, world, and location. On Richard's and Salmon's modifications of Kaplan's view, the truth of a proposition is relative only to a possible world. But relative to a context, a sentence is associated with distinct semantic contents, only one of which is a genuine proposition.

As King (2003) has recently made vivid, the attempts these authors made to repair Kaplan's theory failed. They failed because the semantic theories provided by these authors were not compositional.[4] The mistake Richard and Salmon made was to follow Kaplan in his assumption that tenses and locational operators were operators on time-functional semantic values. There

Kaplan's desired semantics will be irrelevant to our discussion, and in any case is not reflected in his formal system. Also, I ignore the fact that Kaplan (presumably for simplicity's sake) treats contents as relative only to times and worlds in his formal semantics.

[4] Before Richard and Salmon wrote these papers, Lewis (1981) had already noted that the classical notion of a proposition could not be easily assimilated into a compositional semantic theory that treated tenses and locational quantifiers such as 'somewhere' as operators.

is good evidence against the thesis that tenses are operators of any kind, and similar evidence against the thesis that 'somewhere' and other apparent non-modal sentence operators are in fact operators on contents. Instead, tenses appear to be predicates of times, rather than sentence-operators.[5] King (2003) also provides excellent evidence that locational operators are variable-binders, rather than genuine sentence operators. In contrast, there are no decisive reasons to abandon the view that modals are sentence operators. Indeed, one might suspect that modals and attitude verbs are the only genuine sentence operators.[6]

[5] There are several convincing pieces of data against the hypothesis that tenses are sentence operators. First, Partee (1973) argued that we use tenses deictically. An utterance of 'I turned off the stove' is best understood as referring to a particular salient time (say an hour ago), and saying of that time that it was in the past, and I turned off the stove then. This suggests that there is a pronominal temporal element associated with the verb, of which the past tense is a predicate. Secondly, tenses do not significantly iterate, as operators do. The sentence 'Yesterday, I went to the market' does not express the proposition that, in the past of yesterday, I went to the market. Thirdly, consideration of facts about *sequence of tense* is problematic for the operator treatment of tense. For example, there is a natural reading of the sentence 'John saw that Mary was in pain' according to which the seeing and the time of Mary's pain are the same (John saw at *t* that Mary was in pain at *t*, and *t* is in the past). If the past tense contributed an operator, then we should expect only the reading in which John saw that Mary was previously in pain, i.e. at a time previous to his seeing. In contrast, treating the past tense as a predicate of a time produces the desired result (the future tense exhibits only the latter shifted kind of behavior, which is evidence for taking the future tense to be modal (cf. Enç 1996: 349–50)).

[6] This seems to be the conclusion that King (2003) intends. I am sympathetic to it. But it is not necessarily a consensus view among current working semanticists, some of whom reject the thesis that modals are operators (recent work by Angelika Kratzer suggests they may involve object-language quantification over worlds). On another note, Schlenker (2003) has argued, by consideration of various constructions, that attitude verbs are operators on contexts. Though I do not agree with his arguments, given my characterization of 'sentence operator', this position is consistent with the thesis that the only genuine sentence operators are modals and attitude verbs.

We now have the necessary theoretical and historical background in place to present and evaluate different versions of relativism. The key idea behind any version of relativism is that there is a legitimate sense of 'proposition' according to which we may speak of the truth of propositions being relative to judges, or circumstances of assessment. More generally, on any version of relativism, there is a legitimate sense of 'proposition' according to which we may speak of propositions being true relative to certain 'non-standard' features of circumstances of evaluation— that is, features of circumstances of evaluation that go beyond possible worlds and times. Similarly, according to any version of relativism, there is a legitimate notion of propositional truth according to which it is relative to certain 'non-standard' features, such as a judge or a circumstance of assessment (whatever that may be). So, any version of relativism countenances a notion of 'proposition' similar to Kaplan's original gerrymandered contents, a notion that is incompatible with the Fregean thesis that the truth of propositions is absolute, or the more modern concept that the truth of propositions is only relative to possible worlds.

We can distinguish various versions of relativism, according to their degree of departure from the classical conception of proposition and propositional truth (according to which propositions are true or false only relative to possible worlds). The first thesis I will call *radical relativism*.

Radical Relativism
There are no classical propositions and no classical notion of propositional truth. The truth of all propositions is relative to a possible world, together with some non-standard feature, such as a circumstance of assessment, and the truth value of some propositions varies with respect to this non-standard feature.

Radical relativism dispenses with classical truth altogether for the relevant class of propositions. In the case of such propositions, there is truth only relative to a judge, or an assessment.

Radical relativism is the doctrine that our undergraduates espouse, the one that is subject to numerous incoherence objections. If all truth is relative to a judge, or circumstance of assessment, then the doctrine of radical relativism is itself true only relative to a judge. Radical relativism may be true for radical relativist judges, but not true for the rest of us. The worry about appealing to so sweepingly radical a doctrine in the debate over the cases we have been discussing is that it is like denying the law of non-contradiction in order to block someone's argument that one should vote Democratic. It is no point in favor of this doctrine that it may rescue some of our intuitions about knowledge attributions, since it may rescue any pair of conflicting intuitions. As Timothy Williamson (2005) points out about contextualism about truth, 'Charity was never intended to do so much.' Perhaps it is legitimate to defend radical relativism for knowledge as part of a larger defense of the coherence of radical relativism *simpliciter*, but evaluating radical relativism about knowledge apart from a larger discussion of the coherence of radical relativism is not something I can undertake here.

The less radical versions of relativism involve semantic theories somewhat similar to Mark Richard's and Nathan Salmon's revised versions of Kaplan's system. Recall that, on Richard's and Salmon's views, sentences were associated not just with genuine eternal propositions, but also with temporal semantic values. These temporal semantic values were justified by the presence of tense operators that took them as arguments. So, on this view, a sentence was associated with certain semantic contents, relative to a context, that were not genuine propositions. The truth of these tense-logical semantic values was relative to times as well as to possible worlds. These entities were relativist, and so Richard and Salmon did not call them propositions. We could consider these entities to be, if you like, functions from times to genuine propositions.

Similarly, according to what I will call *moderate relativism*, there are genuine (non-relative) propositions, and there is genuine (non-relative) propositional truth. All sentences express relativist propositions, in the sense that the propositions expressed by all sentences are functions from non-standard features of circumstances of evaluation to truth values. But, for most sentences, the relativity to the non-standard features has no semantic effect. Such sentences express *constant functions* from non-standard features of circumstances of evaluation to truth values. Hence, we can take such sentences to express non-relativist propositions (since the relativity has no semantic effect). But, for the moderate relativist, there are classes of sentences that express propositions for which the relativity to non-standard features *does* have a semantic effect. Such sentences express propositions that are non-constant functions from non-standard features of circumstances of evaluation to truth values. Such sentences therefore express genuinely relativist propositions. Furthermore, when we predicate truth of them, we are predicating relative truth of them—namely, truth relative to non-standard features of circumstances of evaluation.

Moderate Relativism
Sentences semantically express relativist propositions; some of these propositions are non-constant functions from non-standard features of circumstances of evaluation to truth values (or genuine propositions). When we predicate truth and falsity of what is expressed by occurrence of sentences, we operate with a relativist notion of truth and falsity.

So, according to moderate relativism, there is a legitimate sense of 'proposition' according to which the propositions expressed by utterances of sentences in that discourse are only ever true relative to worlds and non-standard features of circumstances of evaluation—for example, circumstances of assessment. In problematic cases, our apparently conflicting intuitions are not conflicting, since these relativist propositions are being judged true with respect to different non-standard features of circumstances of evaluation.

The moderate relativist does not deny that there are genuine propositions around, as well as genuine propositional truth (cf. Richard 2004: 230–2). Indeed, I will assume that the moderate relativist can take relativist propositions to be *propositional functions*, functions from the non-standard feature of the circumstance of evaluation to genuine propositions. But, according to her, our intuitions about what is said by utterances of sentences in the relevant discourse track, in the first instance, relativist propositions. Similarly, our intuitions about the truth and falsity of such utterances track their relative truth and relative falsity (relative, that is, to tacitly determined circumstances of assessment).

As I have indicated, moderate relativism does not entail that all discourse is plagued with relativism. According to moderate relativism, the semantic content of any sentence relative to a context is a relativist proposition; say a function from a non-standard feature of a circumstance of evaluation, such as a judge at a time, to either a truth value or a genuine proposition. But, presumably, many sentences, relative to contexts, express *constant* functions from these non-standard features to propositions. In this way, we can distinguish discourse that (by the relativist's lights) tolerates disagreement in which both parties are correct from discourse that does not tolerate disagreement in which both parties are correct. For example, all can agree that the propositions expressed by occurrences of mathematical sentences express constant functions from judges to genuine propositions. There is no relativist resolution of apparent disagreement in this domain.[7]

---

[7] I should distance myself at the outset from the relativist's contention that there can be genuine disagreement in which both parties are correct. Richard (2004: 219) writes about a case in which two people differ over the standards for wealth, and because of that appear to disagree about whether a person satisfies 'is rich': 'It is ... I think ... beyond serious dispute that, even when we recognize that two people differ [in the so-described manner], we take them to have a substantive disagreement ... '. I deplore Richard's contention. Of course the

My purpose in what follows is to evaluate moderate relativism about knowledge ascriptions, the doctrine that the propositions expressed by knowledge ascriptions are non-constant functions from non-standard circumstances of evaluation to genuine propositions. But before I describe this position in greater detail, it is worth looking at one particularly elegant application of the moderate relativist framework, due to Peter Lasersohn (forthcoming). Lasersohn applies the framework to sentences containing predicates of personal taste such as 'fun' or 'tasty'. Lasersohn is correct that predicates of personal taste provide perhaps the best case for a moderate relativist semantic theory. Looking at Lasersohn's semantics (and its motivations) in detail will pave the way for our discussion of moderate relativism applied to knowledge ascriptions.

The purpose of Lasersohn's semantics is to accommodate the intuition that two people may disagree about whether a certain item is fun, but nevertheless both be correct. Lasersohn also seeks to accommodate the behavior of such expressions under operators such as 'for John'. Lasersohn's solution to the problem is to adopt a semantic theory that countenances semantic contents that are analogous to Kaplan's gerrymandered propositions. More specifically, Lasersohn takes the proposition expressed by a sentence such as 'This chili is tasty' to be a set of triples of worlds, times, and what he calls *judges* (or, equivalently, the characteristic function of such a set).

Suppose that John asserts that this chili is tasty and at the same time Mary denies that this chili is tasty. Within Lasersohn's semantics, we can account for the intuition that John and Mary disagree but are both correct. Relative to a context, the content of 'This chili is tasty' is a set of triples of

persons in the so-described situation do not have a substantive disagreement. I similarly regard all talk of the form 'two people genuinely disagree, but they're both right' as absurd. Unfortunately, I will have to adopt such talk occasionally in stating the relativist position.

judges, times, and worlds. Since John asserts this content and Mary denies it, they disagree with one another. But John's utterance of 'This chili is tasty' is true in his context, because what it is for this sentence to be true relative to John's context of utterance is for this chili to be tasty relative to John as the judge. Mary's utterance of 'This chili is tasty' is false in her context, because what it is for this sentence to be true relative to Mary's context of utterance is for this chili to be tasty relative to Mary as the judge. If we construe propositions as sets of the triples relative to which they are true, we can state this in slightly more formal terms. The triple containing John as judge, world w, and time t is a member of the proposition expressed by John's and Mary's uses of 'This chili is tasty'. But the triple containing Mary as judge, world w, and time t is not a member of this proposition.

Lasersohn motivates his semantics by appeal to operators such as 'for John' and 'for Mary'. As Lasersohn points out, we take 'for John' and 'for Mary' to have some kind of semantic effect. One way of smoothly accommodating their semantic effect is by taking them to be sentence operators. But, if they are sentence operators, they clearly do not operate on the world feature of the circumstance of evaluation. That is, the occurrence of 'for John' in 'For John, that chili is tasty' does not have the semantic effect of evaluating the proposition that the relevant chili is tasty relative to another possible world. Instead, the semantic function of 'for John' seems to be to evaluate the semantic content of 'that chili is tasty', at the context of use, *relative to John as the assessor*. This suggests that John himself (and a time of assessment) is a genuine feature of the circumstance of evaluation, one that can be operated on by sentence operators. It suggests, in short, that we think of the truth of the proposition that chili is tasty as relative to judges (at times).

Lasersohn's argument that judges (at times) are genuine circumstances of evaluation is similar to Kaplan's arguments for his gerrymandered contents. As Kaplan (1989: 502–3) writes:

Operators of the familiar kind treated in intensional logic (modal, temporal, etc.) operate on contents. (Since we represent contents by intensions, it is not surprising that intensional operators operate on contents.)...A modal operator when applied to an intension will look at the behavior of the intension with respect to the possible state of the world feature of the circumstances of evaluation. A temporal operator will, similarly, be concerned with the time of the circumstance. If we built the time of evaluation into the contents (thus removing time from the circumstances leaving only, say, a possible world history, and making contents *specific* as to time), it would make no sense to have temporal operators. To put the point another way, if what is said is thought of as incorporating reference to a specific time, or state of the world, or whatever, it is otiose to ask whether what is said would have been true at another time, in another state of the world, or whatever. Temporal operators applied to eternal sentences (those whose contents incorporate a specific time of evaluation) are redundant.

Kaplan's argument for gerrymandered contents concludes from the premise that there are non-redundant temporal operators that times are features of circumstances of evaluation, and propositions are temporally neutral. Similarly, Lasersohn concludes from the premise that 'for John' is a non-redundant operator that judges (at times) are features of circumstances of evaluation, and propositions are neutral with respect to their assessors.[8]

So, Lasersohn takes expressions such as 'for John' and 'for Mary' to be sentence operators, the semantic function of which is to shift the judge index. For Lasersohn, 'for John' works as a temporal operator approach supposes 'At three o'clock' to work. 'For John, this chili is tasty' is true at world w, judge N, and time t

[8] As we saw from the discussion of King (2003), the flaw in Kaplan's argument for his gerrymandered contents is the assumption that tenses are sentence operators, rather than (e.g.) predicates of times. Similarly, one could object to Lasersohn's argument, on the grounds that expressions such as 'for John' in sentences like 'That chili is tasty for John' do not have the semantic function of operators, but have some other function. For example, 'for John' could be part of the specification of the comparison class property for the adjective 'tasty'.

if and only if 'this chili is tasty' is true at world w, judge John, and time t. So the judge element is a genuine feature of the circumstance of evaluation, one that interacts with sentence operators.[9]

Here is the rough idea behind the moderate relativist proposal, as applied to knowledge ascriptions. We take the circumstances of evaluation relative to which a relativist proposition is considered for truth to be a triple of a world, time, and a judge. The proposition expressed by (say) John's utterance of 'I know now that the bank will be open on Saturday' may be true relative to world w, time t, and John as judge, but false relative to world w, time t, and Hannah as judge. Nevertheless, we can account for our intuition that the two are disagreeing when Hannah simultaneously utters 'John doesn't know now that the bank will be open on Saturday'. In the envisaged case, Hannah is in fact denying the same proposition John asserted. So we can account for the intuition, arguably operative in some of the cases discussed in the introduction, that an assertion of knowledge and a denial of knowledge are both true, despite conflicting. For John's utterance expresses a set of ordered triples of worlds, times, and judges, and that is the object that Hannah is denying. Our moderate relativism tells us that our intuitions about truth and falsity of knowledge-ascribing sentences are intuitions about relative truth and falsity, which do not involve a *genuine* clash.

Even if we are temporal eternalists about propositions, and take propositions to be about specific times, we still need another time as a feature of the circumstance of evaluation. For a single judge may change her standpoint of assessment over time. She may be in a Low Stakes situation at one time and a High Stakes situation at a later time. So we need both times and judges as

---

[9] Though I admire the clarity with which Lasersohn executes his proposals, I must confess to not being overwhelmed with the evidence. It is simple enough to elicit the intuition even from the most untutored of subjects that there is no *real* disagreement between someone who maintains that chocolate is tasty and someone who maintains that chocolate is not tasty (unless each is making a claim about what the general public finds tasty).

circumstances of evaluation, even if we take propositions to be about specific times. In fact, we should probably think of the judge and time index as a package, which together yields one non-standard feature of the circumstance of evaluation. In what follows, when I speak of the 'judge index', I will mean the pair of a judge and a time at which that judge is located.

So, according to moderate relativism about knowledge ascriptions, sentences containing the word 'know' express relativist propositions that are non-constant functions from judge indices to genuine propositions. Our intuitions about the truth and falsity of such propositions track intuitions about the relative truth and relative falsity of these propositions. I now turn to an evaluation of this doctrine.

Let us first consider certain epistemic inferences that are constitutive of the knowledge relation. Primary among them is the inference from Kp to p, which we typically call the *factivity* of knowledge. I will argue that the most plausible way to represent the validity of this inference, on the moderate relativist position about knowledge, is still unsatisfactory.

Let $< w, t', x >$ be the relativist circumstance of evaluation, with w the possible world, x the judge, and t' the time at which x is judging. Here are the three clearest ways to represent the factivity of knowledge, on the moderate relativist semantics:

(1) x knows at t that p is true at $< w, t', y >$ only if p is true at $< w, t', z >$ for all z.

(2) x knows at t that p is true at $< w, t', y >$ only if p is true at $< w, t', y >$.

(3) x knows at t that p is true at $< w, t', y >$ only if p is true at $< w, t, x >$.

The first proposal is not satisfactory. According to it, someone can know a proposition relative to a circumstance of evaluation $< w, t', y >$ only if that proposition is true relative to $< w, t', z >$ for all possible judges z. But some judges will be in high-standards situations, such as epistemology classrooms. If the proposition p is itself a knowledge claim, then it is presumably false for some of these high-standards judges (that is, false relative to some $< w, t', z >$). But then one can know only that one knows that q, no matter who the judge is, for propositions q the knowledge of which cannot be undermined by consideration of judges in higher-standard situations. For this reason, the first proposal threatens, for example, to falsify almost all second-order knowledge claims, relative to any circumstance of evaluation.

So the first proposal places untenably restrictive demands on knowledge of one's own knowledge. The second proposal is subject to the following *reductio*. Suppose that John is in a low-standards situation with some evidence for his true belief that p, and Hannah is in a high-standards situation, where more evidence is needed than John possesses in order to know that p. Then, by relativist lights, relative to $< w, t, \text{John} >$, John knows that p, and, relative to $< w, t, \text{Hannah} >$, John does not know that p. This is simply one of the envisaged knowledge relativist accounts of the cases in the Introduction; we have disagreement about whether John knows that p, but both parties are correct.

On the relativist resolution of the intuitions, John and Hannah are each supposed to be vindicated in their respective judgments, despite their genuine disagreement. It is therefore deeply implausible that John and Hannah each is merely lucky to be right. That is, it is not enough that, for John, he is right, and for Hannah, she is right. This is not genuine vindication. It must be that, if they are both correct, then John *knows* that he is right, and Hannah *knows* that she is right. That is, in the envisaged case, John knows that John knows that p, and Hannah knows that John does not know that p. A neutral observer can then point out that John knows that John knows that p, and Hannah knows that John does not know that p (as I have just done). If (2) were correct, it would then follow that John knows that p, and John does not know that p. But that is a contradiction. So (2) is false.

One reply the relativist might give is that what John knows is that, relative to John as judge, John knows that the bank will be open, and what Hannah knows is that, relative to Hannah as judge, John does not know that the bank will be open. If so, then the object of John's and Hannah's respective knowledge state differs, and (2) does not entail a contradiction. However, this is not the relativist position. For the point was supposed to be that John and Hannah *genuinely disagree*. If John and Hannah genuinely disagree, then there is some content about which they both disagree. According to the envisaged reply, they are not genuinely disagreeing, since John maintains that a certain content is true relative to him as judge, and Hannah maintains that it is true relative to her as judge. This is not disagreement.

The third proposal is equally untenable. According to it, if y is the judge, then y's use of 'is true' at time t and world w denotes the property of being true relative to $< w, t, y >$. The third proposal is then consistent with x knowing at t that p, even though p is not true. That is, the third proposal is consistent with x knowing at t that p being true $< w, t, y >$, even though p is false at $< w, t, y >$. This is as straightforward a denial of the factivity of knowledge as one is likely to obtain on this framework.

It is extremely unclear what the factivity of knowledge comes to, on a relativist semantic theory. But any account of the data, no matter what the predictions about particular cases, is more charitable than one that renders mysterious an inference as basic as the factivity of knowledge.

There are other reasons to reject the relativist's semantics for knowledge ascriptions. If knowledge ascriptions do express non-constant functions from judges to truth values or classical propositions (that is, if the relativist about knowledge is correct), then one would expect there to be operators on the judge index that apply to knowledge ascriptions. To see why, let us return to Kaplan's argument for temporalism about propositions, quoted at length above. Kaplan's point is that the existence of non-redundant temporal operators entails temporalism about propositions. If propositions were eternal (that is, not temporally relative), then we should not expect there to be temporal operators at all, since they would have no semantic effect. So, the existence of non-redundant temporal operators is what leads Kaplan to adopt temporalism about propositions.

But suppose that there were no non-redundant temporal operators. There would then be no specifically semantic evidence for temporally relative propositions. Indeed, if there were no non-redundant temporal operators, one would strongly suspect that propositions were eternal. The best explanation of the lack of non-redundant temporal operators would be the fact that there were no suitable contents upon which they could operate, and hence no semantic job for them to do. That is why the emerging consensus that tenses are not operators undermines Kaplan's case for temporalism. Similarly, if there are no sentence operators that operate on the propositions expressed by knowledge ascriptions by shifting the judge feature, the best explanation of the lack of such operators is that they would have no semantic effect. But, if they would have no semantic effect, then that could only be because the propositions expressed by knowledge ascriptions either are not relativist propositions at all, or are constant functions from judges to genuine propositions. In either case, moderate relativism about knowledge would be false.

My argument here bears a certain similarity to an argument by Gareth Evans (1985) for the thesis that descriptions are not referring expressions. Evans first argues that names, pronouns, and demonstratives never switch reference with respect to the possible worlds and times introduced by modal and temporal operators—that is, such expressions are rigid designators.[10] Since definite descriptions do generally behave non-rigidly under modal and temporal embeddings, treating definite descriptions as referring expressions would involve relativizing the reference

[10] If King (2001) is correct, Evans's claim should be restricted to exclude demonstratives.

relation for all expressions to worlds, times, and sequences. Concerning this maneuver, Evans (1985: 190) writes:

This can be done. But it is at a high price, due to the fact that we must relativize the relation of reference in all cases. Simply in order to assimilate descriptions to other referring expressions, we introduce a major change in the semantic apparatus in terms of which we describe the functioning of those other expressions. As a consequence of this change, we ascribe to names, pronouns, and demonstratives semantical properties of a *type* which would allow them to get up to tricks they never in fact get up to; since their reference never varies from world to world, this semantic power is never exploited.

According to Evans, if we relativized the reference relation to worlds and times, we would attribute to names and indexicals semantic flexibility that is not exploited by operators in the language. Since treating definite descriptions as referring expressions would require relativizing the reference relation to worlds and times, we should not treat definite descriptions as referring expressions.

A similar argument could be mounted against the moderate relativist about knowledge who denies that there are any operators that shift the judge index for the propositions expressed by knowledge ascriptions. The moderate relativist would be attributing to such propositions semantic properties that are not exploited by any operators in the language. That would be significant reason to doubt the moderate relativist's claim that such propositions possess such semantic flexibility.

Of course, there is an asymmetry between Evans's argument against relativizing the reference relation to world and times, and my argument against this version of relativism. The asymmetry is that the envisaged relativist holds that we *do* detect the semantic flexibility she imputes to knowledge ascriptions, in our intuitions about the truth and falsity of such ascriptions. But this relativist denies the claim that there are operators in the language that exploit this semantic flexibility. In contrast, in the case discussed by Evans, we never detect the semantic flexibility imputed to names by relativizing the reference relation to worlds and times, even in our truth-conditional intuitions about simple sentences.

But the asymmetry between Evans's argument and my argument is not to the benefit of the relativist about knowledge who denies the existence of relativist content operators. On this version of relativism, there is semantic flexibility to knowledge ascriptions that is reflected in our intuitions about simple sentences. But this semantic flexibility is never reflected in their behavior under operators. This is an extremely odd position. If knowledge ascriptions did have the semantic flexibility imputed to them by the relativist, one would expect there to be operators in the language that exploit it. After all, the very purpose of such semantic flexibility is traditionally to explain embeddings under operators. More generally, the difference between elements of the circumstance of evaluation and elements of the context of use is precisely that it is elements of the former that are shiftable by sentence operators (Lewis 1981). So the position that judges are elements of circumstances of evaluation but cannot be shifted by any sentence operators in the language is an untenable position in the philosophy of language.

So denying the existence of sentence operators that shift the relevant non-standard feature of the circumstance of evaluation is not a tenable position for the moderate relativist about knowledge. On the other hand, it is hard to see how the moderate relativist about knowledge could countenance the existence of such operators, if she is to preserve her claim to be providing a more charitable account of our intuitions about knowledge ascriptions. Suppose $O\text{-}j$ is an operator on the judge feature, one that evaluates the content of the embedded sentence at the judge feature corresponding to j. Then, the moderate relativist would countenance the truth of claims such as '$O\text{-}j$ John knows that the bank will be open, but not $O\text{-}h$ John knows that the bank will be open'. I cannot think of any natural language stand in for such operators that are linked to some notion of truth, and would make it acceptable to countenance the truth of instances of these claims.

We can of course imagine someone truly uttering 'According to John, John knows that the bank will be open, but not according to Mary'. But 'according to John' and 'according to Mary' in this construction are not linked to any notion of truth, relativist or otherwise. These constructions just mean that, if asked, John would accept the claim that he knows that the bank will be open, but Mary would reject this claim. Appeal to the intuitive truth of such constructions is not an aid to the person who wishes to argue that there are operators that express relative *truth*.

More importantly, as we saw in the case of Ludlow's argument for contextualism in Chapter 3, expressions such as 'by low standards', 'by high standards', and 'by the standards of chemistry' can occur appended to virtually any predication. Furthermore, as we also saw, such expressions can occur appended to conjunctions of knowledge ascriptions with non-epistemic sentences. If such expressions expressed operators on judges, then *all (non-mathematical) discourse would be relativist*. Thus, if the relativist about knowledge took such expressions to be operators on judges, she would be led to be a relativist about all empirical discourse.

Here is why the relativist cannot take expressions such as 'by the standards of chemists' to express epistemic content operators on judges, without adopting relativism about all empirical discourse.[11] Consider any discourse like the following:

(4) By the standards of chemists, the stuff in the Hudson River isn't water, and someone with no lab experience doesn't know that hydrogen is an element.

[11] The discussion here is reminiscent of the discussion of Ludlow in Chapter 3, but applied to relativism.

What (4) shows is that expressions such as 'by the standards of chemists' can append to conjunctions of knowledge ascriptions and non-epistemic discourse. It is deeply implausible to maintain that 'by the standards of chemists' has differing effects on the first conjunct and the second conjunct. Whatever effect 'by the standards of chemists' has on the knowledge ascription in the second conjunct of (4), it has the same effect on the first conjunct of (4). If the effect of 'by the standards of chemists' is to evaluate the second conjunct with respect to judges that hold a higher epistemic standard, then it has the same effect on the first conjunct. So, the relativist who takes such expressions to express operators on judges would then be led to take 'the stuff in the Hudson river isn't water' to express a non-constant function from judges to genuine propositions or truth values. Since one can imagine similar conjunctions with virtually all empirical discourse, this would show that virtually all empirical discourse is relativist. The relativist about knowledge would therefore be ill advised to take 'by low standards' and 'by high standards' as operators on judges.

So there are many reasons to think that the relativist about knowledge, of whatever variety, is not in possession of a more charitable account of our intuitions about various knowledge attributions than the contextualist or the advocate of IRI. Considerations of charity aside, however, there is a more overarching reason to be suspicious of relativism (of either the radical or the moderate variety). According to the relativist, truth is relative to a parameter that is distinct from the parameters with which we are familiar (for example, worlds and times). But the direction of research in linguistics has suggested that there are fewer and fewer parameters with respect to which truth is relative; perhaps the only such parameters are possible worlds (cf. King 2003). So postulating more and more such parameters seems to be swimming against the tide of history.

In the light of the above, the advocate of some alternative to IRI and standard contextualism is perhaps best advised not to advance any version of relativism at all. Though it is often unclear what doctrine apparent advocates of relativism intend to promote, it is possible to read some of them as instead advocating a non-standard version of contextualism. On this version of non-standard contextualism, judges are not features of circumstances of evaluation, but are heretofore unrecognized elements of the context of use. Since they are unrecognized elements of the context of use, we use the terms 'what is said' and 'proposition' perhaps unknowingly to refer to the semantic value of a sentence relative to the other members of the contextual index, but still unsaturated by the judge index.

This version of non-standard contextualism aids the contextualist against certain kinds of criticisms. For example, Hawthorne (2004: 98 ff.) argues that contextualism makes some odd predictions about propositional attitude reports. If, however, there are legitimate senses of phrases such as 'proposition', 'what is said', and 'what is believed' that denote entities that are not genuine propositions, then perhaps the contextualist could evade some of Hawthorne's criticisms, as well as some of the criticisms I have provided above. For example, Hawthorne (2004: 103) objects to the contextualist that:

there is no reading available of
  (5) You believe that you know that you have feet.
      which corresponds to
  (6) You believe that you know-by-your-standards that you have feet.

But the non-standard contextualist can respond by arguing that ordinary belief attributions link believers not to genuine belief contents, but rather to the proposition expressed by the relevant sentence, relative to that context, minus the element determined by the judge index.

I have some sympathy with the claim that phrases such as 'what is said' and 'what is believed' can occasionally be used to refer to entities that are not propositional (see Stanley (1997: 577) for examples in which these phrases denote semantic values that are neutral concerning both time and place). But to respond to the objections Hawthorne and I have leveled against contextualism, the non-standard contextualist requires a stronger thesis than simply that 'what is said' and 'what is believed' and 'proposition' *can* be used to refer to the result of leaving out the element determined by the judge index from the proposition semantically expressed by the sentence. Hawthorne's claim above is that there is *no* reading available of (5) according to which it expresses (6). Similarly, my objection that contextualism is committed to delivering an incorrect result for zoo was that there is *no* reading of this discourse in which it could be true. To defend against these objections, the non-standard contextualist cannot simply rest content with the thesis that 'what is said', 'what is believed', and 'proposition' *can* be used to refer to non-propositional entities in the disputed cases. She must argue that such expressions can *never* be used to refer to genuine propositions in the disputed cases.

Though there is evidence that expressions such as 'what is said' can sometimes be used to refer to non-propositional entities, there is no evidence, from consideration of uncontroversial context-sensitivity, that these expressions *cannot* be used to refer to the result of saturating the semantic content of the sentence with whatever contextual element is at issue. For example, while there is evidence (Stanley 1997) that 'what is said' can be used to refer to something that is temporally neutral, there is no evidence that 'what is said' *cannot* be used to refer to something that has its time built into it—that is, a genuine eternalist proposition. Since the non-standard contextualist faces criticisms that involve discourses that can *never have* the readings that contextualism predicts they could have, the non-standard contextualist is committed to the very strong claim that 'what is said' and 'what is believed' can never refer, in the disputed cases, to the semantic entities produced by resolving all contextual dependence. This is a prima facie implausible semantic claim, since there is just no parallel for it elsewhere in the language.[12]

Finally, in my discussion of standard contextualism, I provided many objections that have nothing whatever to do with propositional attitude reports, or the use of expressions such as 'what is said' or 'what is believed'. Non-standard contextualism is of no help to the contextualist in evading these sorts of objections. So I am skeptical about the existence of a version of non-standard contextualism that will overcome the problems of contextualism.

My aim in this chapter has not been to refute relativism about knowledge (though I believe it to be false). The relativist about knowledge (of whatever stripe) argues that relativism helps evade the problems facing the contextualist and the interest-relative invariantist. My purpose has been to show that relativism is far from an unproblematic alternative to contextualism and IRI. Indeed, our discussion suggests that it raises far more questions than it answers. The move to the dramatic sounding new semantic position, while perhaps promising in other domains (for example, predicates of personal taste), has no obvious benefits in the case of knowledge.

In the next chapter I turn to some topics outside epistemology, but with bearings on the dispute between the doctrines we have been discussing. Contextualism has been applied to many debates outside epistemology. I have argued that one virtue of IRI is that it is not, like contextualism and relativism, a blanket solution to all cases of apparent conflict throughout philosophy. Rather, IRI is plausible in the epistemological case only because of special

[12] One may perhaps read Richard (2004) as attempting to provide support for it, by appeal to certain features of comparative adjectives. But he does not succeed in establishing the very strong claim that one cannot refer, with the use of 'what is said' or 'what is believed', to the result of saturating the semantic content even with the sort of contextual values he is discussing.

features of knowledge. This strengthens IRI, as against context-ualism and relativism, since it suggests that IRI is a specifically epistemological doctrine, rather than a general method of evad-ing apparent conflicts, applicable everywhere.

8

Contextualism, Interest-Relativism, and Philosophical Paradox

My purpose in this final chapter is to look at some attempts to apply context dependence and interest-relativity to problems outside epistemology. I focus on the case of vagueness, and, in particular, on appeals to contextualism or interest-relativity in the resolution of the sorites paradox. The reason for the focus on the sorites paradox is that, unlike the case of the liar paradox, there are prima facie acceptable accounts of these paradoxes along both contextualist and interest-relative lines. So, while I will have comments to make in passing about some of the (by now large) literature on context-sensitive approaches to the liar paradox, my focus here is on appeal to context-dependence in the resolution of some natural versions of the sorites paradox.

According to what I will call a *contextualist* solution to the sorites paradox, vague terms are context-sensitive, and one can give a convincing dissolution of the sorites paradox in terms of this context-dependency. The reason, according to the contextualist, that precise boundaries for expressions like 'heap' or 'tall for a basketball player' are so difficult to detect is that, when two entities are sufficiently similar (or saliently similar), we tend to shift the interpretation of the vague expression so that, if one counts as falling in the extension of the property expressed by that expression, so does the other. As a consequence, when we look for the boundary of the extension of a vague expression in its penumbra, our very looking has the effect of changing the interpretation of the vague expression so that the boundary is not where we are looking. This accounts for the persuasive force of sorites arguments.

Suppose we are presented with fifty piles each of which has one grain less than the pile to its left. On the far left is a pile we are strongly inclined to call a heap when presented alone. This pile is in the definite extension of 'heap'. On the far right is a pile we are slightly inclined not to call a heap when presented alone. It is towards the end of the penumbra of 'heap'. But starting with the left-most pile (pile 1), we may make progressive judgments of the form:

(a) If that pile 1 is a heap, then pile 2 is a heap.
(b) If pile 2 is a heap, then pile 3 is a heap.
(c) Etc.
(d) Etc.
(n) If pile 49 is a heap, then pile 50 is a heap.

Each of these conditionals would be one to which we would assent. By agreeing to this succession of conditionals, we eventually come to pile number 50, which we now would strongly feel inclined to count as a heap. The explanation for this, according to the contextualist, is that, as we are presented with each conditional, the two piles are sufficiently similar so as to cause us to interpret 'heap' in such a way to count one as a heap if and only if the other is a heap. This has the effect of changing the property expressed by 'heap' as we progress through the series of conditionals.[1]

---

[1] The contextualist solution faces something of a problem with conditionals, the antecedent of which concerns the last member of the penumbra

Before we evaluate the conditionals, the property expressed by 'heap' may exclude the last ten piles from counting in the extension of 'heap'. But once we start to evaluate the conditionals, the boundary for 'heap' changes. And that is why a boundary between the heaps and the non-heaps is undetectable. Wherever we look, it is not there.

In this chapter, I will argue that the contextualist account of the sorites paradox is problematic; I will also show how some of my arguments extend to undermine certain contextualist accounts of the liar paradox. I then turn to a close cousin of the contextualist account of the sorites, the *interest-relative* theory of vagueness advocated by Graff (2000). On Graff's view, vague terms are one and all context-sensitive, but not in a way that the contextualist believes. Graff's view evades the objections I give against the contextualist. In the second half of the chapter, I argue that the mechanisms that allow Graff's interest-relative view to evade the problems facing the contextualist land her theory in perhaps more intractable difficulties. I conclude by returning to the epistemological doctrine of Interest-Relative Invariantism (IRI), showing why the problems that arise for Graff's interest-relative account of vagueness do not arise for IRI.

Scott Soames, a prominent advocate of contextualism about vagueness, states the contextualist position on the semantics of vague expressions as follows:

To say that vague predicates are context sensitive is to say that they are indexical. While the semantic content of an indexical varies from one

of a vague term, and the consequent of which concerns the first member of the determinate anti-extension. Some of her principles would lead her to count the consequent as true, while others would lead her to reject the consequent as false (essentially, those principles that are sensitive to the similarity between the two cases would rule in favor of the truth of the consequent, whereas the principles that require the members of the definite anti-extension never to be in the extension of the term in any context would rule in favor of its falsity). This problem is raised in Robertson (2000). For Soames's reply, see Soames (2002: 443–4 n. 13).

context of utterance to another, its meaning does not. Rather its context-invariant meaning constrains the indexical to take on semantic contents with certain specified features. Sometimes these constraints identify semantic content in terms of a fixed contextual parameter— e.g. the content of 'I' is the agent of the context, the content of 'now' is the time of the context, and the context of 'actually' is the world of the context. In other cases, the meaning of an indexical constrains its semantic content to be one that satisfies a certain condition—e.g. the content of 'he' must be male, the content of 'she' must be female, and the content of 'we' must be a group of individuals that includes the agent of the context. A speaker using one of these indexicals is free to select any salient content that satisfies the relevant constraints.

If, as I believe, vague predicates are context-sensitive, then this is the model on which they must be understood.[2]

So, on the contextualist theory, each vague term is an indexical, like 'I', 'here', and 'now'.[3]

Here is a fact about indexical expressions. Indexicals have invariant interpretations in verb-phrase ellipsis (henceforth, VP ellipsis). So, for example, consider:

(1) John likes me, and Bill does too.
(2) Hannah lives here, and Bill does too.
(3) Hannah is supposed to be in Syracuse now, and Mary is too.
(4) John saw Hannah's film, and Bill did too.
(5) John read that, and Bill did too.

---

[2] Soames (2002: 445). Other prominent contextualist theories include Kamp (1981) and Raffman (1994, 1996). It is not clear to what degree Tappenden's influential (1993) counts as a contextualist theory, in the sense in which I have defined it here.

[3] To be more exact, the contextualist aspect in Soames's theory (1999) is intended as a solution of the dynamic or particularized version of the sorites paradox, where speakers are confronted with a sorites series over a period of time. Other aspects of Soames's views play a more central role in addressing generalized versions of the sorites paradox. I will be considering only particularized versions of the sorites paradox in this chapter.

There is no available interpretation of (1) in which John and Bill are said to like different people. This is so, even if the person who uttered the second conjunct of (1) is different from the person who uttered the first conjunct. Similarly, there is no available interpretation of (2) according to which Hannah and Bill are said to live in different places, and no interpretation of (3) according to which Hannah and Mary are supposed to be in Syracuse at different times. (4) cannot be uttered with the intention of expressing the proposition that John saw the film Hannah produced, while Bill saw the film Hannah directed. Finally, if one utters the first conjunct of (5) while demonstrating one object, say a book, the second conjunct must be understood expressing the proposition that Bill read that self-same book, even if one is pointing at a different book when uttering the second conjunct.[4]

When a pronominal expression has a non-invariant interpretation in VP ellipsis, this signals that a higher operator binds it. So, consider:

(6) John loves his mother, and Bill does too.

Suppose, in uttering (6), the speaker is pointing at Tim, and hence using 'his' demonstratively. In this case, (6) can only mean (7). But if 'his' is a pronoun anaphoric on 'John', then (6) can mean (8):

(7) John loves Tim's mother, and Bill loves Tim's mother.
(8) John loves John's mother, and Bill loves Bill's mother.

The standard account of this ambiguity is that the logical form of the verb phrase in (6), when read as (8), is '$\lambda x(x$ loves x's mother)'. This predicts reading (8) of (6), since (6), at logical form, is then:

---

[4] The one exception to this generalization about indexicals occurs with the discourse: 'I love you. [response] I do too.' This does not work with verbs other than 'love'.

(9) John $\lambda x(x$ loves x's mother), and Bill $\lambda x(x$ loves x's mother).

In sum, when an expression is used indexically or demonstratively, then it has an invariant reading under VP ellipsis. If, in contrast, it is used as an anaphor, then it is bound by a higher operator, and may give rise to non-invariant readings.[5]

According to the contextualist, a vague predicate has a character that determines different properties in different contexts. So, the content of a vague predicate must be invariant in VP ellipsis. But this raises problems in accounting for all versions of the sorites paradox. For consider the following version of the paradox. Suppose we are presented with a series of n piles of grains. The $n+1$th heap in the series of piles has one less grain than the nth heap. The first member of the series clearly is a heap, and some grains that clearly do not suffice to make a heap form the nth member of the series. Suppose, ostending each pile of grains in turn (where 'that$_j$' is a demonstrative used to refer to the jth heap in the series), we say either:

(10) That$_1$ is a heap, and that$_2$ is too, and that$_3$ is too, and that$_4$ is too, ... and that$_n$ is too.

(11) If that$_1$ is a heap, then that$_2$ is too, and if that$_2$ is, then that$_3$ is, and if that$_3$ is, then that$_4$ is, ... and then that$_n$ is.

The contextualist presumably wishes to claim that the reason each conjunct in (10) and each conditional in (11) is so compelling is that the similarity between the ith member of the series and the i^{+1th} member of the series causes us to adjust the content of 'heap' so that its extension includes both. But, since VP ellipsis is

---

[5] As Ludlow (1989) and Stanley (2000) emphasize, comparison classes for comparative adjectives are best thought of as the values of variables in logical form that can be anaphorically controlled by higher operators (see Ch. 3 n. 3). So, in 'That elephant is small, and that flea is too', the logical form is something like 'that elephant $(\lambda x \lambda Y(x$ is small for $Y))$, and that flea $(\lambda x \lambda Y(x$ is small for $Y))$', where the 'Y' argument is saturated by the common noun.

used in this version of the sorites, this strategy cannot succeed. If the word 'heap' is an indexical, then it does not shift its denotation in any of the different conjuncts in (10) or any of the different conditionals in (11). Since no context shifts are possible in these cases, the contextualist's semantic account fails to explain why we find each step in (10) and (11) so compelling.

The sorites paradox does not just arise for nouns such as 'heap'. For example, consider the verb 'shout'. One might suppose that, if someone is shouting, then someone who is speaking a tenth of a decibel less loudly is also shouting. Suppose we start by considering someone who is clearly shouting, and in turn hear a series of people, each of whom is speaking a tenth of a decibel less loudly than the previous person. Then, we can say:

(12) If she$_1$ is shouting, then she$_2$ is too, and she$_3$ is too, and she$_4$ is too . . .

Here, too the contextualist would have to maintain that the verb 'shout' changes its content in the successive occurrences of VP ellipsis. But, as we have seen, this is semantically implausible. Similar particularized versions of the sorites paradox can be constructed for prepositions, such as 'near' and 'far'.

I emphasize the importance of the fact that the sorites paradox can be constructed across every syntactic category to dissuade objectors from attempting to respond to the above arguments by appeal to features specific to a particular syntactic category. For example, Stanley and Szabo (2000) defend the thesis that nouns are syntactically associated with domain indices, whose interpretation can be controlled or bound by higher elements. Exploiting this framework might allow someone to provide an explanation of the shiftability of the interpretation of nouns under VP ellipsis, since one could argue that the index associated with each noun is controlled by a different operator associated with the verb phrase. Since we can produce a parallel argument from VP ellipsis for terms of each syntactic category, this maneuver is plausible only as a response to the problematic, if it can be argued to generalize across the board. But no one has begun to make the argument that the sort of considerations discussed by Stanley and Szabo (2000) and Stanley (2002) generalize to expressions of every syntactic category (that is, that each term has a syntactically active contextual variable associated with it). But this is what we would need, if we were to extend this line of defense against the VP ellipsis argument across the board.

So, the contextualist cannot explain these versions of the sorites paradox. But neither can she give a distinct explanation of (10)–(12). For, presumably, we find each conjunct in (10) and (12) (and each conditional in (11)) compelling for the very same reason that we find each step in a normal sorites series compelling. There is no plausibility to a disjunctive explanation of these cases.

Any response the contextualist gives must be consistent with the fact that switching interpretations under VP ellipsis is not possible with other indexicals. For example, suppose Hannah, Mark, Sally, and Bill are in my office. Pointing to each in turn, I utter:

(13)   Hannah is here, and Mark is too, and Sally is too, and Bill is too.

In (13), the content of 'here' cannot shift under the VP ellipsis. For example, the space I indicate with 'here' cannot expand as I proceed down the sequence. So any appeal to special mechanisms that allow 'heap' to shift its interpretation in (10) and (11), and 'shout' in (12), must be consistent with the fact that 'here' cannot shift its interpretation in (13).

Nor is there plausibility in the claim that we reinterpret the original use of 'heap' or 'shout' with each successive VP ellipsis. First, in the case of (13), the successive VP ellipses do not allow the speaker to widen successively the original denotation for 'here'. Secondly, this response seems inconsistent with the phenomenology of the case. We certainly seem to be using the ellipsis to make anaphoric reference to a property we have been attributing all along to other piles of grains. Finally, contextualism is intended as a *semantic* solution to the sorites. The solution is supposed to be that vague terms are semantically context-sensitive. The semantic content of each elided phrase in the examples in (10)–(12) is determined by the semantic content of the initial use of the term, rather than any alleged reinterpretation of it. There is thus no contextualist semantic solution that treats all of these cases.

Intuitively, here is the problem versions of the sorites like (10)–(12) pose for the contextualist account. Owing to the use of VP ellipsis, the property expressed by the vague term in question must be the same across the different stages of the sorites series. But contextualist solutions account for the force of the sorites by appealing to a change in the property expressed. This explanation does not work for these examples.

Ellis (2004) has recently objected to the above arguments, on the grounds that we can imagine the following case:

Thirty friends are standing in the middle of a very large field. One of them has the following idea: 'Why don't we each go stand in any place we choose, and see where everyone goes. Jill, you go first.' Jill walks a good distance away from the group and shouts, 'I'm going to stand here!' It's Tom's turn next, and being the tag-along Tom is, he goes straight for Jill and stands right next to her. Jill exclaims humorously, 'And I guess Tom is too!' Sally then goes and stands on the other side of Jill, who now says 'And apparently, so is Sally!' Then Bill goes and stands behind Jill ('and so is Bill'), and then Ann stands in front of Jill ('and Ann') . . . In this case, the interpretation of 'here', which appears in VP ellipsis, varies. We can imagine that had the second person (Tom) gone and stood where the 30th person ended up, Jill would not have said, 'And I guess Tom is too!'

Ellis's point is to argue that indexicals can after all shift under VP ellipsis. But Ellis's example does not support his conclusion. Ellis's example is a clear case of a particularized sorites series, for the predicate 'is here'. Ellis shows that, via consideration of a particularized sorites series, one can establish an unintuitive conclusion involving a use of this predicate. But it is hard to see why this is an interesting result.

Like uses of any vague predicate, insofar as one is tempted to say that uses of 'heap' are *tolerant*, one is equally tempted to say that uses of 'is here' are tolerant, in the sense that a small difference does not matter (if x is here, and y is two inches away, then y is here too), and so are sorites susceptible. My point was of course not to argue that vagueness does not affect indexical expressions. My point was rather that one cannot dissolve the sorites series by appeal to features of indexical expressions; vagueness remains even when indexicality goes away. Ellis's case clearly shows that indexical predicates are vague. But that is a conclusion fully in accord with my view that indexicality cannot explain vagueness, not in opposition to it.

Considerations from VP Ellipsis also pose problems for some contextualist accounts of the liar paradox, such as that defended in Burge (1979). According to Burge, the predicate 'true' is an indexical, like 'here' or 'now'. Relative to a context c, 'true' is to be thought of as denoting the property of being *true$_i$* for some level i (think of these as levels of the Tarskian hierarchy). Using this theory, Burge claims to resolve the liar paradox.

Burge splits the derivation of the liar paradox into several distinct steps:

Step (a) (1) (1) is not true.
Step (b) (1) is not true (because *pathological*).
Step (c) (1) is true after all.

Burge evades the paradox, by arguing that in step (a) and (b) 'true' is interpreted as true$_i$, whereas in step (c) 'true' is in fact interpreted as true$_j$, for some $j>i$. Burge gives three distinct characterizations of *pathologicality$_i$*; that is, pathologicality relative to a level i. On all of them, a sentence may be pathological$_i$, but not pathological$_j$ (and may indeed be true$_j$) for some $j>i$. Crucially, on all of them, sentences that are pathological$_i$ are not true$_i$. On the simplest such characterization, all and only sentences containing 'true$_k$' for $k \geq i$ are pathological$_i$, as in Tarski's work. So, the three steps of the derivation of the liar paradox are:

Step (*a*) (1) (1) is not true$_i$.
Step (*b*) (1) is not true$_i$ (because pathological).
Step (*c*) (1) is true$_{i+1}$.

Steps (*b*) and (*c*) are fully consistent. Different properties are ascribed to (1). The paradox is blocked.

It is crucial to Burge's account that the truth predicate is a true indexical (a 'narrow indexical', in the sense of Stanley (2000: 411)), one that cannot be bound by higher quantifiers. For, if the alleged context-sensitivity of the truth predicate were due to the fact that the index associated with 'true' could be bound by higher quantifiers, it would be simple to produce instances of the liar paradox that could not be resolved via Burge's strategy, as in:

(14) For all *j*, this sentence is not true$_j$.
(15) This sentence is not true at any level.

As Burge (1979: 192) notes:

The indexical-schematic character of semantical predicates cannot be formally obviated by adding an argument place—relativizing them to a language, a level, a context, or a viewpoint. For quantification into the argument place will provide an open sentence just as subject to paradox as the 'naïve' truth-predicate formalization.... Attempts to produce a 'Super Liar' parasitic on our symbolism tend to betray a misunderstanding of the point of our account. For example, one might suggest a sentence like (*a*), '(*a*) is not true at any level'. But this is not an English reading of any sentence in our formalization. Our theory is a theory of 'true', not 'true at a level'. From our viewpoint, the latter phrase represents a misguided attempt to quantify out the indexical character of 'true'; it has some of the incongruity of 'here at some place'. No relativization will 'deindexicalize' 'true'.

So, Burge is certainly committed to the true indexical character of 'true'.

But there are other properties of true indexicals, aside from their inability to be bound by higher quantifiers. In particular, as we have seen, indexicals cannot shift their content in VP ellipsis. We may use this feature of true indexicals to show that Burge has no account of the force of some perfectly ordinary presentations of the liar paradox. One example of an instance of the liar paradox that resists Burge's true indexical treatment is:

> (16) This sentence is not true. So it is not the case that the sentence just mentioned is true. So it is.

Another is displayed by the following sort of reasoning:

> (1) (1) is not true.
> (1) is not true (because pathological).
> So, (1) is.

Burge cannot reject these sentences as non-English, as he does with the attempt to quantify over levels. The sentences in (16) are perfectly well formed. But if 'true' is an indexical, as Burge requires it to be, then they are instances of the liar paradox that Burge's theory cannot explain.[6]

Let us now return to the contextualist account of the particularized sorites paradox. As we have seen, considerations from VP ellipsis raise the worry that appeal to indexicality does not resolve the paradox. Further problems for the contextualist account come from considerations of modal embeddings. In particular, the contextualist account makes incorrect predictions about versions of the sorites paradox that involve counterfactual conditionals. Consider

---

[6] These objections are specific to Burge's version of contextualism about the truth predicate. They do not straightforwardly apply to the versions of contextualism about the truth predicate that follow the suggestions of Parsons (1974)—for example, as developed in Glanzberg (2001, 2004).

(17) Patch P1 is red. That would still be true even if P1 were indistinguishably more orange than it is. And that would still be true even if P1 were indistinguishably more orange than that . . . And that would still be true even if P1 were indistinguishably more orange than that. But then it would be clearly orange. Contradiction.[7]

According to the contextualist account, 'red' is an indexical expression. So its content is fixed in context. Subsequent propositional anaphora on the content of 'Patch P1 is red' is then fixed by the content of 'red' relative to the context of use of the first sentence in (17). So, if the contextualist is correct, (17) should seem much less compelling than an ordinary particularized sorites series. But (17) is just as compelling as any other version of the sorites paradox.

So, we have seen two kinds of problems for the contextualist account of the particularized sorites paradox, one from VP ellipsis, and the other from modal contexts. Both constructions allow us to construct versions of a particularized sorites series that have no resolution on the envisaged account (and so these examples are analogous to the problem 'strengthened liar' sentences raise for various accounts of the liar paradox). This motivates consideration of another style of theory.

Though she does not consider the above sort of worries for contextualist accounts, Delia Graff (2000) nevertheless provides an account of the sorites paradox that shares many of the virtues of the contextualist account just canvassed, but that promises to evade its problems. Graff does not explain the force of the sorites by appeal to vague expressions having different semantic contents in different contexts. On Graff's view, in the course of a sorites series, each occurrence of a vague term has the same content as the other occurrences. However, in the course of

---

[7] Thanks to Richard Heck for help with replacing my earlier attempt to formulate this worry with this superior version.

a sorites series, the *extensions* of the univocal property expressed by the different occurrences of the vague term differ. Let me explain.

Consider a sentence such as:

(18) That mountain is tall for a mountain.

Graff adopts the degree theoretic treatment of gradable adjectives developed in Kennedy (1999). According to it, 'tall' denotes a measure function, a function from objects to degrees on a scale (in this case, a scale of height). According to Kennedy, in the syntax of a sentence such as (18), there is an absolute morpheme that combines with the measure function denoted by 'tall' to yield a function from individuals to truth values. The function takes an individual x to be true just in case the degree of height of that individual (the value of tall(x)) is at least as great as the contextually salient degree of height.

To treat the phenomenon of vagueness, Graff proposes adjusting the meaning of Kennedy's absolute morpheme, so that it means *significantly greater than*, rather than *at least as great as* (see Graff 2000: 74). She also makes the meaning of 'significantly greater than' relative to persons (ibid.: 75). Abstracting from irrelevant details, on Graff's theory, where x is a person (most naturally taken to be the person who utters the sentence), relative to a context, the proposition expressed by an occurrence of (18) is:

(19) That mountain has significantly greater height for x than the typical height for mountains.

So, in short, Graff's theory exploits Kennedy's account of adjectives, replacing Kennedy's *at least as great as* relation by her *significantly greater than for* x relation.[8]

---

[8] Graff is admirably explicit about the syntax and semantics of her proposal. However, as she recognizes, the cost of her explicitness is that her proposal faces the worry that it does not generalize to expressions that are not gradable adjectives. For example, no one has ever suggested that in the syntax of nouns

As Graff points out, her proposal involves 'less context dependency' than contextualist accounts of the sorites. Consider the predicate 'significant to Tony Blair'. This predicate is *not* context-sensitive. It always expresses, as Graff points out, the same *interest-relative property*. However, since what is in fact significant to Tony Blair changes over time (and across worlds), the univocal property expressed by this predicate changes its extension over time (and across worlds). But this change in extension is due to a change in the facts at different times, not due to features of the context of use of the predicate. Similarly, the predicate 'is a US Citizen' changes its extension over time, though it always expresses the same property, and so is not context-sensitive.

It is instructive to see why Graff needs to relativize the relation expressed by 'significantly greater than' to persons. If she did not, then the proposition expressed by (18) would be that that mountain is significantly greater than the typical height of mountains. But then no truth value for this proposition would be determined given a time and a world. For a time and a world pair is too *large* to determine what is significant. Relative to this universe now, there are simply too many conversations occurring to fix on a unique set of interests. So Graff's strategy requires that one needs to relativize the relation to a particular person or persons, at that time and world. So Graff's theory is not an entirely interest-relative account. There is still some context-sensitivity associated with a vague expression. But once one fixes upon a person or persons whose interests are at stake,

---

such as 'heap' there is a constituent expressing a greater-than relation, as has been suggested in the case of adjective phrases. But, as I have previously emphasized, one's account of the force of the sorites for nouns should be the same as one's account of the force of the sorites for comparative adjectives. There is no plausibility to a thoroughly disjunctive account of the force of the sorites, one for nouns, one for verbs, and one for comparative adjectives. So it is in fact a very serious worry with Graff's proposal that it is not clear how to generalize it to nouns and verbs.

subsequent uses of the vague expression all express the same property (significant for that person).

Here is how Graff's theory accounts for the force of the sorites. Consider a series of people. On the far left is a man who is clearly tall for a typical British man. On the far right is someone clearly not tall for a typical British man. To the immediate right of the man on the far left is a person one millimeter shorter than he is, and to his right is a man one millimeter shorter than he is, and in general, to the right of each man in the series is someone one millimeter shorter than he is, a series stretching until the man on the far right. For each pair of men x and y standing next to one another, we are inclined to accept the conditional:

(20) If x is tall, then so is y.

Suppose one person, Hannah, is successively considering all of the conditionals of the form (20). Unlike contextualist solutions, Graff's account implies that the property expressed by 'tall' in such a context does not shift when Hannah considers the truth value of these successive conditionals. In each case, it expresses the interest-relative property of being, for Hannah, significantly taller than the typical British male. But, since Hannah considers these conditionals *at different times*, what counts as significant for Hannah changes at these different times. So, the extension of the interest-relative property of being, for Hannah, significantly taller than the typical British male changes during the course of her consideration of the different conditionals. So, while the contextualist explanation appeals to shifts in the property expressed by a vague term across contexts to explain a change in extension, Graff's interest-relative account of vagueness appeals to a change in time (circumstance of evaluation) to explain the change in extension, despite no change in the property expressed.

Assuming that Graff can somehow extend her interest-relative semantics to noun and verb denotations, she has no problem with a sorites series such as (10), (11), or (12). For her, the property expressed by the elided VP is exactly the same property as was expressed by the initial use of the vague expression. Since it is an interest-relative property, the property has a different extension relative to different times, varying as a function of the relevant person's interests. So, her account of a sorites series involving VP ellipsis is simply exactly the same as her account for a sorites series not involving VP ellipsis.[9]

Graff's theory also has no problems with the versions of the sorites that involve counterfactual conditionals. Since, on her view, vague terms express properties that concern interests, what will be relevant to fixing the extension of a vague term relative to another possible situation will be the interests we would have in that other possible situation. This yields a satisfactory, uniform account of versions of the sorites such as (17).

Graff's theory correctly reflects the sense that, when one person evaluates a sorites series, the force of the series has nothing to do with a shift in the property expressed by the vague term. However, in order to capture these data, Graff incurs some extremely strong commitments about the propositional content of occurrences of sentences containing vague terms. In particular, since, on her view, vague expressions express interest-relative properties, propositions expressed by occurrences of sentences containing them are what one might call interest-relative propositions. Such propositions are about *persons and their interests*. The sense in which the propositions expressed by occurrences of sentences containing vague terms are

---

[9] Instances of the schema 'x is [F] too' involve an anaphoric presupposition, about something previously mentioned, that it is F, in addition to x being F. The tense of the instance of 'x is F too' filters down to the presupposition, so that the presupposition is that the previously mentioned thing is, at the very same time as x is said to be F, also F. But this does not pose a problem for a Graffian account of a sorites series like (10). The previously mentioned instance is also in the new extension of the property at the later time.

about persons and their interests is as strong as it can be. As Graff (2000: 75) writes:

Significantly greater than is a context-dependent relation, since what is significant to one person may not be significant to another. Any use of 'significant', or of any word whose content involves what is significant, requires an implicit subject with interests—an answer to the question: *significant to whom?*

Graff's point here is that 'significant' is what is sometimes called a 'relational word', one that involves implicit anaphora. For those who accept Russellian conceptions of propositions, it should be uncontroversial that the propositions expressed by sentences containing relational expressions that involve implicit anaphora contain, as constituents, the objects or properties in question.[10] For example, consider the relational word 'enemy', and the proposition expressed by (18), as uttered by Bill:

(21) John is an enemy.

Like 'significant', the word 'enemy' involves an implicit argument; an enemy is *an enemy of* x, for some contextually understood *x*. The propositions expressed by sentences containing 'enemy' contain the implicit argument as a constituent. For example, the proposition expressed by this occurrence of (21) is that *John is an enemy of Bill*. Had Bill not existed, what is expressed by (21) could not be true. Similarly, no one could believe what is expressed by (21) without having a belief about Bill.

According to Graff, in the syntax of sentences containing comparative adjectives, there is an expression, Kennedy's absolute morpheme, that is to be understood as the *significantly*

---

[10] It should also be uncontroversial that the sentences containing expressions involving implicit arguments contain syntactic elements whose value, relative to a context, is the implicit argument. For example, this position can be bound ('Most people have a significant other'). But this additional commitment is somewhat more controversial, involving, as it does, differing views about the nature of syntax (see Partee 1989; Stanley 2000).

greater than relation. So, the absolute morpheme is a relational expression, like 'enemy'. As a consequence, its implicit argument, relative to a context, is a constituent of the proposition expressed by sentences containing it, relative to that context. So, in particular, the propositions expressed by sentences containing comparative adjectives, for Graff, contain, as constituents, the individual or individuals whose interests are at issue.

But this is problematic. Suppose John utters:

(22) Mount Everest is tall for a mountain.

According to Graff, this occurrence of (22) expresses the proposition that Mount Everest is significantly for John taller than the typical mountain. But what (22) expresses could still be true, even if John had never existed (and hence did not have interests or purposes). Furthermore, one can easily believe what is expressed by (22) without having a belief about John. This suggests, *contra* Graff, that there is no expression in the syntax of sentences containing comparative adjectives that is relative to the interests of persons.

Even if the implicit argument of the *significantly greater than* relation were not a constituent of the proposition expressed by (22), there would still be a serious worry for Graff. For, even if there were no people, and hence no significant interests at all, what is expressed by an occurrence of (22) could still be true. But it is difficult to see how the proposition expressed by occurrences of (22) on Graff's account could be true in such a circumstance.

In a similar vein, there are instances of the sorites paradox, such as Wang's Paradox, that involve necessarily existing objects and properties that presumably are essential to them. For example, the number 3 is small, and it seems to us plausible that, if n is small, then so is $n + 1$. Any account of the force of the sorites paradox must explain these as well. But the proposition expressed by '3 is small' is true, even in possible situations in which there are no significant interests.

One response Graff could give to these problems would be to *rigidify* on the significant interests of the person in question. The aim of this tactic would be to have the above envisaged occurrence of (22) express something like:

(23) Mount Everest is actually for John significantly greater in height than the typical mountain.

If this tactic is successful, then perhaps the modal pressure on Graff's proposal would be alleviated. For what (23) expresses could be true in a world in which John does not exist, since what would be relevant in that world is whether Mount Everest bears the actually significantly-greater-than-for-John relation to the height of the typical mountain in that world.[11]

However, this rigidification strategy does not free Graff from the problems. First, it robs Graff of an advantage her theory has over the contextualist. For it leaves her in the same position as the contextualist with respect to versions of the sorites like (17). Secondly, it does not help with the most serious problem facing her view. In order to believe what is expressed by an occurrence of (22) with John as the speaker, one does not need to believe anything so fanciful as (23). One can believe what is expressed by such an occurrence of (22), without having beliefs about either John or what is significant to him, and one can believe what is expressed by such an occurrence of (22) without having any beliefs about the value of the rigidifying operator 'actually' (see Soames (1998) on rigidified definite descriptions). So Graff's proposal gives an inadequate account of the content of the propositions expressed by sentences containing vague terms.[12]

---

[11] Thanks to Delia Graff for this suggestion. An independent worry about this strategy, which I will not develop, is that it is not clear how to rigidify. Where does the actually operator occur in the syntax?

[12] Here is another worry for Graff's proposal, due to Timothy Williamson (p.c.). Consider a version of the sorites paradox the major premise of which is 'For all x, y, and t, if x is tall at time t, and y is one millimeter shorter than x at t,

As we evaluate a sorites series, according to the contextualist, the property expressed by a vague term changes as the context of evaluation changes. But such accounts cannot explain the force of a sorites paradox where the semantic mechanisms postulated by the contextualists are inoperative. Since a uniform account of the force of the sorites is desired, contextualist solutions are problematic. Graff's interest-relative account can give the desired uniform account of these cases, because her account of the sorites does not involve the property expressed by a vague term changing as one proceeds down the sorites series. But, to achieve this result, she must enrich the properties expressed by vague terms with information about persons and their interests, which has highly counter-intuitive consequences in modal and epistemic contexts. So it seems that neither contextualist nor interest-relative accounts of the force of sorites satisfactorily explain its grip.

The worries I have raised for Graff's account of vagueness do not arise in the case of IRI. One worry we have raised for Graff is that, on her theory, it seems that the propositions expressed by sentences containing vague terms—that is, most propositions ordinarily expressed—are only true relative to worlds that contain persons or their interests. The fact that the proposition that Mount Everest is a tall mountain could be true even with respect to a world in which human life had never formed is a significant blow to Graff's theory. However, a comparable objection is not forthcoming in the case of IRI. The proposition expressed by an occurrence of an instance of 'N knows that p' could only be true

---

then y is tall at t'. It is not clear how to extend Graff's proposal to meet this version of the paradox, where the time of evaluation is explicit. However, Graff may respond by arguing that the *significantly greater than for x* relation has a temporal element that is potentially distinct from the temporal element associated with 'tall' (or the copula), and instances of this universal generalization will involve different times associated with the *significantly greater than for* x relation. There are problems with this response, but I will not pursue these issues here.

relative to worlds in which *N* exists. In contrast, the proposition expressed by an occurrence of 'Mount Everest is a tall mountain' could be true, even if the person or persons whose interests are at issue had never existed. Similarly, while someone could believe the proposition expressed by an occurrence of 'Mount Everest is a tall mountain' without having any beliefs about the person uttering the sentence, no one could believe the proposition expressed by an occurrence of 'John knows that he has hands' without having a belief about John.

Finally, as Graff recognizes, a purely interest-relative account is no more available in the case of vagueness than it is in the case of the liar paradox. To make an interest-relative account even partly plausible, we have to incorporate certain dependencies upon context (for example, to the person or persons involved in the conversation). So, a pure interest-relative account is in any case not on offer for the case of vagueness. In sum, it is certain specific features of knowledge attributions that make them amenable to an interest-relative account. Interest-relativity, unlike contextualism, is not a broad-based strategy to cast at any apparent philosophical conflict.

9

Conclusion

I have argued in this monograph that knowing is an interest-relative relation. Whether or not someone's true belief at a certain time that *p* is an instance of knowledge depends in part upon non-truth-conducive factors. The conclusion is bolstered by the intuitive connections between knowledge and action, revealed in certain intuitions we have about when someone knows and when someone does not know. I have considered and rejected the most plausible alternative account—namely, contextualism about knowledge ascriptions. I have also shown that the claim that knowledge is an interest-relative notion is not just a blind application of a general strategy, applicable to every philosophical dispute. Rather, it is motivated by special features of the case of knowing, not present in the case of other philosophical paradoxes.

As I have indicated in Chapter 6, there are two interestingly conflicting morals that one could draw from the fact that knowledge is an interest-relative notion. The first moral is that the interest-relativity of knowledge shows that epistemologists should be concerned not with knowledge, but rather with epistemically pure notions of *evidence* and *justification*. If knowledge is interest-relative, but evidence and justification are not, then epistemology should be the study of the latter two notions, and not the former 'corrupted' notion. Those sympathetic to this moral may want to employ it to counter the powerful arguments of Williamson (2000) that epistemologists should focus on 'knowledge first', and notions such as evidence and justification are ultimately to be explicated in terms of it. If knowledge is interest-relative, but evidence and justification are not, then, *contra* Williamson (2000: ch. 9), my evidence at a time cannot be what I know at that time.

The reader will be forgiven for thinking at times that my sympathies lie with the advocates of this first moral. In Chapter 5, when I explicated a version of Interest-Relative Invariantism about knowledge, I did so with the use of a first-order theory of knowledge that appeared to employ only non-interest-relative notions of evidence. On that account, practical interests helped determine the amount of evidence one needed to have in order for a true belief to be knowledge, where amount of evidence was modeled with the use of epistemic probability. On this account, it appears that the role of practical interests is just to 'set' the level of evidence one needs to possess, where evidence itself is not an interest-relative notion.

It is, however, important to bear two points in mind about my particular development of IRI in Chapter 5. First, my interest in this monograph does not lie in advancing a first-order theory of knowledge. Rather, my purpose has been to establish a connection between knowledge and practical interests, one that any correct account of knowledge must respect. The reason I developed a first-order account of knowledge was just to show how one sample account of knowledge in terms of evidence could incorporate the interest-relativity of knowledge. Secondly, the key notion I employed in the particular first-order theory I selected to develop along interest-relative lines was *epistemic probability*. As I indicated in Chapter 5, I am dubious that epistemic probability is a notion that is 'knowledge free', in the sense that a full account of the nature of epistemic probability could be given without appeal to knowledge. The interest-relativity of knowledge therefore makes the interest-relativity of epistemic probability more likely, rather than less.[1]

These points lead us to the second and opposing moral that may be drawn from the fact that knowledge is an interest-relative notion. It is prima facie difficult to accept that one person knows that p and another does not, despite the fact that they have the same evidence for their true belief that p. But, if knowledge is anywhere near as central to epistemology as the considerations in Williamson (2000) suggest, then one would expect that evidence is similarly interest-relative. If so, one's practical situation will affect the evidential standing one has with respect to one's belief that p, and not just whether one knows that p. On this view, the interest-relativity of knowledge does not entail that two people can differ in what they know, despite sharing the same evidence.

If evidence and related epistemic notions are similarly interest-relative, then there may be no *purely epistemic notions*, in the sense of a notion that is 'stripped clean' of its ties to the practical interests of epistemic agents. In the face of this situation, one might appeal to a Carnapian 'rational reconstruction' of a purely epistemic notion of justification or of knowledge. Attempts to do so will be hindered by the concern that any such purified notion will not play the familiar roles we ask of our ordinary epistemic concepts. It may turn out that part of the value of these concepts comes in the links they have to our practical interests. Finally, if all of our epistemic notions share the connections to practical interests that knowledge possesses, it will be very difficult to tell when we have successfully produced a notion purified of such links.

Some of the considerations I have supplied in this book can be used to support the interest-relativity of other epistemic notions

[1] I stop short of concluding that the interest-relativity of knowledge entails the interest-relativity of epistemic probability, because one of the morals of Chapter 4 is that properties of properties that feature in the analysis may not be properties of the analysandum.

besides knowledge. Furthermore, as I have indicated, my own view is that all epistemic notions are interest-relative. Nevertheless, I have focused my arguments on establishing the interest-relativity of knowledge, and thus the central arguments of this book are consistent with either moral.

REFERENCES

Burge, Tyler (1979). 'Semantical Paradox', *Journal of Philosophy*, 76: 169–98.

Cappelen, Herman and Lepore, Ernie (2005). *Insensitive Semantics* (Oxford: Blackwell).

Cohen, Stewart (1988). 'How to Be a Fallibilist', in J. Tomberlin (ed.), *Epistemology* (Philosophical Perspectives, 2, Atascadero, CA: Ridgeview), 91–123.

—— (1991). 'Skepticism, Relevance, and Relativity', in Brian McLaughlin (ed.), *Dretske and his Critics* (Cambridge, MA: Blackwell).

—— (1999). 'Contextualism, Skepticism, and the Structure of Reasons', in J. Tomberlin (ed.), *Epistemology* (Philosophical Perspectives, 13; Oxford: Blackwell), 57–89.

—— (2000). 'Contextualism and Skepticism', in E. Sosa and E. Villaneuva (eds.), *Skepticism* (Philosophical Issues, 10), 94–107.

DeRose, Keith (1991). 'Epistemic Possibilities', *Philosophical Review*, 100/4: 581–605.

—— (1992). 'Contextualism and Knowledge Attributions', *Philosophy and Phenomenological Research*, 52/4: 913–29.

—— (1995). 'Solving the Skeptical Puzzle', *Philosophical Review*, 104: 1–52.

—— (1996). 'Knowledge, Assertion, and Lotteries', *Australasian Journal of Philosophy*, 74: 568–80.

—— (1999). 'Contextualism: An Explanation and Defense', in J. Greco and E. Sosa (eds.), *The Blackwell Guide to Epistemology* (Oxford: Blackwell), 187–205.

—— (2000). 'Now You Know It, Now You Don't', *Proceedings of the Twentieth World Congress of Philosophy*, v. *Epistemology* (Bowling Green, OH: Philosophy Documentation Center), 91–106.

DeRose, Keith (2002). 'Assertion, Knowledge, and Context', *Philosophical Review*, III: 167–203.

—— (2004). 'Single-Scoreboard Semantics', *Philosophical Studies*, 119/1–2: 1–21.

—— (forthcoming). 'The Ordinary Language Basis for Contextualism and the New Invariantism', *Philosophical Quarterly.*

Dretske, Fred (1970). 'Epistemic Operators', *Journal of Philosophy*, 67: 1007–23.

—— (1981). *Knowledge and the Flow of Information* (Cambridge, MA: MIT Press)

—— (2000). 'The Pragmatic Dimension of Knowledge', in Dretske, *Perception, Knowledge, and Belief: Selected Essays* (Cambridge: Cambridge University Press).

Ellis, Jonathan (2004). 'Context, Indexicals, and the Sorites', *Analysis*, 64/4: 362–4.

Enç, Mürvet (1996). 'Tense and Modality', in Shalom Lappin (ed.), *The Handbook of Contemporary Semantic Theory* (Oxford: Blackwell), 345–58.

Evans, Gareth (1985). 'Reference and Contingency', in *Collected Papers* (Oxford: Clarendon Press), 178–213.

Fantl, Jeremy and McGrath, Matthew (2002). 'Evidence, Pragmatics, and Justification', *Philosophical Review*, III/1: 67–94.

Feldman, Richard (1999). 'Contextualism and Skepticism', in J. Tomberlin (ed.), *Epistemology* (Philosophical Perspectives, 13; Oxford: Blackwell), 93–115.

Frege, Gottlob (1979). 'Logic', in *Posthumous Writings*, ed. H. Hermes, H. Kambartel, and F. Kaulbach, trans. Long and White (Chicago: University of Chicago Press), 126–51.

Gauker, Christopher (2003). *Words without Meaning* (Cambridge, MA: MIT Press).

Gillies, Anthony (forthcoming). 'Shifty Epistemology'.

Glanzberg, Michael (2001). 'The Liar in Context', *Philosophical Studies*, 103: 217–51.

—— (2004). 'A Contextual-Hierarchical Approach to Truth and the Liar Paradox', *Journal of Philosophical Logic*, 33: 27–88.

Goldman, Alvin (1976). 'Discrimination and Perceptual Knowledge', *Journal of Philosophy*, 73 (1976), 771–91.

Graff, Delia (2000). 'Shifting Sands: An Interest-Relative Theory of Vagueness' *Philosophical Topics*, 28/1: 45–81.

Halliday, Dan (forthcoming). 'Contextualism, Comparatives, and Gradability', *Philosophical Studies*.

Harman, Gilbert and Sherman, Brett (2004). 'Knowledge, Assumptions, Lotteries', *Philosophical Issues*, 14: 492–50.

Hawthorne, John (2004). *Knowledge and Lotteries* (Oxford: Oxford University Press).

Heller, Mark (1999). 'Contextualism and Anti-Luck Epistemology', in J. Tomberlin (ed.), *Epistemology* (Philosophical Perspectives, 13; Oxford: Blackwell), 115–29.

Joyce, James (2002). 'Levi on Causal Decision Theory and the Possibility of Predicting One's Own Actions', *Philosophical Studies*, 110: 69–102.

Kamp, H. (1981). 'The Paradox of the Heap', in U. Monnich (ed.), *Aspects of Philosophical Logic* (Dordrecht: Reidel).

Kaplan, David (1989). 'Demonstratives', in Joseph Almog, John Perry, and Howard Wettstein (eds.), *Themes from Kaplan* (Oxford: Oxford University Press), 481–63.

Kennedy, C. (1999). *Projecting the Adjective: The Syntax and Semantics of Gradability and Comparison* (New York: Garland Press).

King, Jeffrey (1998). 'What is a Philosophical Analysis?' *Philosophical Studies*, 90: 155–79.

—— (2001). *Complex Demonstratives: A Quantificational Account* (Cambridge, MA: MIT Press).

—— (2003). 'Tense, Modality, and Semantic Value', in John Hawthorne and Dean Zimmerman (eds.), *Language and Philosophical Linguistics* (Philosophical Perspectives, 17; Oxford: Blackwell).

Klein, Peter (2000). 'Contextualism and Academic Skepticism', *Philosophical Issues*, 10: 108–16.

Kratzer, Angelika (1977). 'What "Must" and "Can" Must and Can Mean', *Linguistics and Philosophy*, 1: 337–55.

Lasersohn, Peter (forthcoming). 'Context Dependence, Disagreement, and Predicates of Personal Taste'.

Lewis, David (1981). 'Index, Context, and Content', in Stig Kanger and Sven Ohman (eds.), *Philosophy and Grammar: Papers on the Occasion of the Quincentennial of Uppsala University* (Dordrecht: D. Reidel), 79–100.

—— (1983). 'Scorekeeping in a Language Game', in Lewis, *Philosophical Papers* (New York: Oxford University Press), i. 233–49.

—— (1996). 'Elusive Knowledge', *Australasian Journal of Philosophy*, 74: 549–67.

Ludlow, Peter (1989). 'Implicit Comparison Classes', *Linguistics and Philosophy*, 12: 519–33.

—— (2005). 'Contextualism and the New Linguistic Turn in Epistemology', in G. Preyer and G. Peters (eds.), *Contextualism in Philosophy*, (Oxford: Oxford University Press).

MacFarlane, John (2005a). 'The Assessment Sensitivity of Knowledge-Attributions', in T. Gendler-Szabo and J. Hawthorne (eds.), *The Oxford Guide to Epistemology*.

—— (2005b). 'Making Sense of Relative Truth', in *Proceedings of the Aristotelian Society*.

Moore, G. E. (1993). *Commonplace Book 1919–1953* (Bristol: Thoemmes Press).

Neta, Ram (2003). 'Contextualism and the Problem of the External World', *Philosophy and Phenomenological Research*, 66: 1–31.

—— (forthcoming). 'Contextualism and a Puzzle about Seeing', *Philosophical Studies*.

Nunberg, G., Sag, I., and Wasow, T. (1994). 'Idioms', *Language*, 70: 491–538.

Parsons, Charles (1974). 'The Liar Paradox', *Journal of Philosophical Logic*, 3: 381–412.

Partee, Barbara (1973). 'Some Structural Analogies between Tenses and Pronouns in English', *Journal of Philosophy*, 70: 601–9.

—— (1989). 'Binding Implicit Variables in Quantified Contexts', in C. Wiltshire, B. Music, and R. Graczyk (eds.), *Papers from CLS 25*: 342–65 (Chicago: Chicago Linguistics Society).

Raffman, D. (1994). 'Vagueness without Paradox', *Philosophical Review*, 103/1: 41–74.

—— (1996). 'Vagueness and Context-Sensitivity', *Philosophical Studies*, 81: 175–92.

Richard, Mark (1981). 'Temporalism and Eternalism', *Philosophical Studies*, 39: 1–13.

—— (1982). 'Tense, Propositions, and Meanings', *Philosophical Studies*, 41: 337–51.

—— (2004). 'Contextualism and Relativism', *Philosophical Studies*, 119/1–2: 215–41.

Robertson, T. (2000). 'On Soames's Solution to the Sorites Paradox', *Analysis*, 60/4: 328–34.

Rysiew, Patrick (2001). 'The Context-Sensitivity of Knowledge Attributions', *Nous*, 35/4: 477–514.

Salmon, Nathan (1986). *Frege's Puzzle* (Cambridge, MA: MIT Press).

—— (1989). 'Tense and Singular Propositions', in Joseph Almog, John Perry, and Howard Wettstein (eds.), *Themes from Kaplan* (Oxford: Oxford University Press), 331–92.

Schaffer, Jonathan (2004). 'From Contextualism to Contrastivism', *Philosophical Studies*, 119/1–2: 73–103.

Schiffer, Stephen (1996). 'Contextualist Solutions to Skepticism', *Proceedings of the Aristotelian Society*, 96: 317–33.

Schlenker, Philippe (2003). 'A Plea for Monsters'. *Linguistics and Philosophy*, 26: 29–120

Soames, Scott (1986). 'Incomplete Definite Descriptions', *Notre Dame Journal of Formal Logic*, 349–75.

—— (1998). 'Wide Scope and Rigidified Descriptions', *Nous*, 32: 1–22.

—— (1999). *Understanding Truth* (New York: Oxford University Press).

—— (2002). 'Replies', *Philosophy and Phenomenological Research*, 429–52.

Stanley, Jason (1997). 'Names and Rigid Designation', in B. Hale and C. Wright (eds.), *A Companion to the Philosophy of Language* (Oxford: Blackwell), 555–85.

—— (2000). 'Context and Logical Form', *Linguistics and Philosophy*, 23/4: 391–434.

—— (2002). 'Nominal Restriction', in G. Peters and G. Preyer, *Logical Form and Language* (Oxford: Oxford University Press), 365–88.

—— (2005a). 'Fallibilism and Concessive Knowledge Attributions', *Analysis*, 65/2: 126–31.

—— (2005b). 'Semantics in Context', in Gerhard Preyer and G. Peter (eds.), *Contextualism* (Oxford: Oxford University Press).

—— and Szabo, Z. (2000). 'On Quantifier Domain Restriction', *Mind and Language*, 15: 219–61.

—— and Williamson, T. (1995). 'Quantifiers and Context-Dependence', *Analysis*, 55: 291–5.

—— —— (2001). 'Knowing How', *Journal of Philosophy*, 90/8: 411–44.

Stine, Gail (1976). 'Skepticism, Relevant Alternatives, and Deductive Closure', *Philosophical Studies*, 29: 249–61.

Tappenden, J. (1993). 'The Liar and Sorites Paradoxes: Toward a Unified Treatment', *Journal of Philosophy*, 90: 551–77.

Unger, Peter (1975). *A Case Study for Skepticism* (Oxford: Oxford University Press).

Vogel, Jonathan (1999). 'Relevant Alternatives Theory', in J. Tomberlin (ed.), *Epistemology* (Philosophical Perspectives, 13; Oxford: Blackwell), 155–80.

Wettstein, Howard (1984). 'How to Bridge the Gap between Meaning and Reference', *Synthese*, 58: 63–84.

Williamson, Timothy (2000). *Knowledge and its Limits* (Oxford: Oxford University Press).

—— (2005). 'Contextualism, Subject-Sensitive Invariantism, and Knowledge of Knowledge', *Philosophical Quarterly.*

Yourgrau, Palle (1983). 'Knowledge and Relevant Alternatives', *Synthese*, 55: 175–90.

INDEX